Patio Produce

Visit our How To Website at www.howto.co.uk

At www.howto.co.uk you can engage in conversation with our authors – all of whom have 'been there and done that' in their specialist fields. You can get access to special offers and additional content but most importantly you will be able to engage with, and become a part of, a wide and growing community of people just like yourself.

At www.howto.co.uk you'll be able to talk and share tips with people who have similar interests and are facing similar challenges in their lives. People who, just like you, have the desire to change their lives for the better – be it through moving to a new country, starting a new business, growing their own vegetables, or writing a novel.

At www.howto.co.uk you'll find the support and encouragement you need to help make your aspirations a reality.

For more information on growing vegetables on your patio and other small spaces, visit www.patio-produce.co.uk.

How To Books strives to present authentic, inspiring, practical information in their books. Now, when you buy a title from **How To Books,** you get even more than just words on a page.

Patio Produce

How to cultivate a lot of
home-grown vegetables from
the smallest possible space

Paul Peacock

Spring Hill

Published by Spring Hill

Spring Hill is an imprint of How To Books Ltd
Spring Hill House, Spring Hill Road,
Begbroke, Oxford, OX5 1RX, United Kingdom
Tel: (01865) 375794 Fax: (01865) 379162
info@howtobooks.co.uk
www.howtobooks.co.uk

How To Books greatly reduce the carbon footprint of their books by sourcing their typesetting and printing in the UK.

First edition 2009

British Library Cataloguing in Publication Data
A catalogue record for this book is available from the British Library

ISBN: 978 1 905862 28 3

Cover illustration by Sam Tickner of Firecatcher Creative
Text illustrations by Rebecca Peacock
Cover design by Baseline Arts Ltd, Oxford
Produced for How To Books by Deer Park Productions, Tavistock
Typeset by TW Typesetting, Plymouth, Devon
Printed and bound by Bell & Bain Ltd, Glasgow

CONTENTS

PREFACE

There is a huge interest in growing vegetables and food. A recent survey suggested that five million people wanted to 'live the good life' and keep chickens, grow some of their own food and somehow achieve a level of self sufficiency.

But many of us believe the idea of getting anywhere near self sufficient can only be a distant dream because we live in the city. We have a balcony thrusting into the sky from a city centre flat, a 'back yard' as we say in the north, on a terraced house of the tiniest patio area there is. This belief is erroneous. *Patio Produce* aims to show the reader in simple practical terms just how much is possible in the smallest space.

If you have access to sunlight, you can grow at least some of your own food, and in this world of globalisation, where our produce is flown in from the far corners of the earth, growing your own has some amazing consequences.

Firstly, you are helping to save the planet. Even in a small way the journey from your patio or balcony or the path to your door to your plate is metres and not hundreds of kilometres. That has to have an environmental payoff.

Secondly, you can grow without chemicals, and in this book we make the point that using chemicals on the patio might bring problems not thought of compared to wider use in the garden and on a farm. You can be completely sure the food you grow is healthy, fresh food.

The food you grow in pots, containers, bags and grow bags can be the best food ever. I remain convinced that potatoes taken from their compost, cooked and consumed within minutes of them being in the ground and growing, have a flavour no gourmet, no chef, no restaurant can beat.

More than any of these reasons for growing your own, regardless of what space you have, no way of life is healthier for anyone than to get compost under your fingernails and see green things growing. Don't sit frustrated at the space you have; don't give up before you even start. Get out there and grow something.

This book is meant to be handled, scribbled on, tried out, watered by accident and generally dirtied by grubby fingers. It is a book to be dipped into when you need information and read whole when you need a little inspiration. I have grown all of the plants and produce over the years in the tiniest of situations and I can say they really do work – even in the north of England where I live.

Paul Peacock

CHAPTER 1

THE ENVIRONMENT OF THE PATIO

This book is aimed at the majority of us who live in terraced houses, high rise flats, town houses and semi-detached properties with little more than a postage stamp for a garden and often nowhere to grow but the patio.

It seems the great buzz words of the last few years are 'Grow your Own'. A real movement of people who grow their own food is building in popularity and I longed to be one of them. But with no land at all and even less free time, the whole idea of growing vegetables seemed dead in the water. I became increasingly frustrated watching TV gardeners with acres of space, room for tonnes of produce, chickens and pigs, tell me how easy it was to live off the land. Television programmes that exhorted me to get out there and 'Dig for Victory' simply got on my nerves.

I tried an allotment but it had insurmountable problems for me. It was too far away for a start; by the time I got there it was time to come home. Secondly, there were too many regulations. There was always someone coming along with something negative to say (I have since found out that the politics of the allotment can sometimes be difficult to cope with). Finally, when I tried to find a 'friendlier' allotment I found there were no plots available; nothing but waiting lists. So, finally I cut my losses and decided to concentrate on turning my little postage stamp of a patio into a productive food-producing machine.

WHY BOTHER GROWING ON A PATIO?

So, why should we bother growing our own vegetables on a patio when there isn't that much space there in the first place?

We have all been urged to look inside our shopping baskets to find out where our food comes from, what chemicals are in them, how many food miles they have travelled and what are the rights and wrongs of the stuff we eat. One thing that all the pundits seem to be agreed on is that sooner or later we will have to grow more of our own food at home. The economics of shipping tomatoes from Kenya and potatoes from Brazil will eventually give way to a more home grown, local system of growing and distributing food. But even if you care little for the politics of food, the very idea of having fresh produce at your back door must excite anyone who, like me, likes their grub. Once you have tasted potatoes plucked from your own garden, carried to your kitchen, cooked and eaten within minutes, you will no doubt have all the motivation needed for growing more and more food at home, even if there is only a postage stamp's space to grow it in.

The common patio takes many shapes and is made from all sorts of material. For some, like those in a modern town house, it is simply a few paving slabs dropped by the French windows. For others it is a raised area of decking, and for some it is a balcony many metres in the air. The environment of the patio, the growing conditions and its ability to sustain plant life obviously depends on the geographical setting, but they all have some properties in common. There are many reasons why you should consider patio gardening techniques in your garden if it is less than around 10m^2. In such a small garden there is not really enough space to set aside land for crops, and by growing in containers you will have a greater versatility, the ability to move crops around, and by harvest, probably a better yield.

THE BASICS OF GROWING IN POTS AND CONTAINERS

There is no end to the ways you can grow on a patio, and no end to the crops you can grow. Of course, the very word patio implies that you will actually be growing in pots and containers of all kinds. Containers should provide all the requirements for a plant to grow well, if only for a few days at a time and with the added bonus of being able to move them around to suit your needs. As a plant grows too large for a space you can move it elsewhere, or you can rotate your pots so that the plants might get their turn of good sunlight.

WATER, ROOTS AND SHOOTS

Roots, the parts of plants we normally don't see, need to be kept healthy. Healthy roots do not always make for healthy shoots, but the opposite is always the case. Containers need to be the correct size for the plant so that the roots can grow without being confined. The compost they grow in needs to provide water and oxygen as well as an ample supply of nutrients and support so the plant doesn't fall out of the pot in the breeze. Sometimes in growing on the patio it is necessary to help the roots by providing extra support.

Plants are very selective about where they grow. Too much water and you will find most roots begin to rot, not enough and you will find the plant drying up. The first tip for growing on the patio is **water little and often**, rather than copiously and infrequently.

When a plant becomes waterlogged the problem is the lack of oxygen. The plant can get what it needs from water but when this is used up, the oxygen dissolved in the water is also used up and isn't replaced. What you are looking to provide is a balance between a film of water to coat the root hairs and a good air space for oxygen to pass through the water and into the plant.

Soil drainage

Do all you can to maintain the drainage of the pot. Make your own compost or growing medium by mixing with sand; normally I find 30% sand and 70% compost is ideal and put a few pebbles or broken crockery in the bottom of the pot. The sand is there to improve the drainage and the compost to act as a sponge to hold water. Sometimes you will want to grow in material that resembles neither soil nor compost. Carrots, for example, grow well in sand with a little vermiculite thrown in, then fed inorganically with liquid feed.

Sharing water

On the whole, the patio does not get the same benefit from rainfall as the full-sized garden. Water not collected in the pots that lie about the patio is lost to the plants because it simply runs away. In the garden, soil acts as a huge sponge distributing moisture evenly to all the plants, but the roots of the pot-grown plant cannot share in the next pot's water. Consequently, patio crops are thirsty even when it rains, and you should implement a regime of watering for most days. Experience will show which plants need watering most, but take it as a golden rule that they need more than those in the ordinary garden.

Because you have to water pots and containers more frequently than the ordinary garden, the nutrients in the soil tend to wash out with any excess. The systems that circulate nutrients in the soil cannot work inside a pot, so they need feeding more frequently to make up that which is lost. Use slow release fertiliser where you need it most (they are more expensive and should be used only with hungry plants) and have a ready supply of compost for topping up. If you can manage to water with a weak solution of fertiliser, all the better.

WHAT POTS AND CONTAINERS YOU WILL NEED FOR GROWING PRODUCE ON A PATIO

You will need a range of pots from tiny modules no bigger than your thumb for sowing seeds, to 40cm pots or larger for small trees. I have always found it important to have a range of pot types, clay, plastic and more modern materials like polystyrene. I also make a lot of pots out of paper for seedlings and burying into containers.

If you are putting pots on the floor of the patio then always position them on pot stands where possible, and if you cannot, raise them on a stone or a piece of wood, anything to raise them off the ground. This will avoid the pot freezing to the ground on the coldest days and it is much easier to deal with pests like slugs and snails – but more of this later.

Grow bags

Conventional pots are not the only way of growing on the patio. You can buy and make all manner of receptacles for plants. Grow bags are excellent for a number of reasons as long as you remember to put drainage holes in them. Grow bag quality is directly proportional to their cost. I buy cheap ones which I lay alongside paths and in these I grow salad crops. Because I steal most of my 'land' from the path, they take up very little room and thankfully, the days when we have to push a child's buggy along the path are long gone.

Laid flat grow bags can produce lettuce, beets, spring onions, cucumbers, radish and baby carrots all along my path. However, you can put the grow bag on its end and open the top to grow a variety of crops. Carrots grown in this way are superb. They are long and thick and fantastically tasty – but there are other ways to grow big carrots on the patio explained later in the book. You can grow potatoes this way too, if you are desperate, but there are hundreds of ways of growing potatoes.

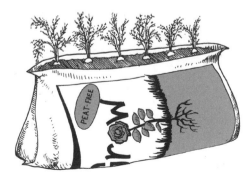

Fig. 1. Carrot growbag

Plastic bags

The ordinary, maligned plastic bag from the supermarket is very versatile on the patio. You can hang them up by their handles and use them as an impromptu hanging basket, or you can run a rope or washing line through the handles and line them up in mid air. I find this to be almost the ideal way of growing turnips. They are also good at lining larger planters, which while we are on the subject can be made from any old wood – I find a ready supply of wooden pallets to be really helpful.

By tearing them into strips and knotting, you can crochet supermarket bags together to make a large, very strong container that will hold big pots, hanging basket style, or you can fashion them into a large container itself to grow crops directly. This kind of structure makes for excellent potato growing bags.

Larger bags, those you get with stones or sand delivered from a builder's merchants, make fantastic stand-alone planters, particularly for potatoes and you can get half a ton of potatoes in one of those bags, but also for cabbages, cauliflowers and sprouts. Their size makes it possible to grow carrots while at the same time affording sufficient protection from carrot root fly. This type of bag can also be painted in acrylic or emulsion to brighten up or tone in the bag to the surroundings.

Sports bags

Every rugby season, I go through about three sports bags. They simply don't stand up to the abuse of muddy rugby boots for two training sessions, a match on Saturday and refereeing on Sunday. The old bags make great containers for growing potatoes; they're black, they're rugged and they leak. To be honest I thought the bag smelled of potatoes before I started planting. One thing led to another and I tried growing spuds in the bag with great success.

THE BEST WAY TO GROW PATIO PLANTS

By copying nature and growing in clusters, the success of your patio produce will be improved no end. If you line up your plants in pots and containers you will get good growth, but you can enhance the growing space and the enjoyment of your garden by growing in clusters. You can entice plants to grow more naturally by copying how they might be found in nature. For a start, if you place a number of pots and planters together in a huddle you can maximise the effect of rain. A raindrop missing one plant is more likely to water another. You can improve the possibilities of insect pollination by growing together plants bees might be interested in. You can improve a tranquil Sunday summertime siesta by putting together aromatic plants that make the air healthily refreshing, and plonking your deckchair in the middle of them. This makes it much easier to protect a discrete number of plants from the ravages of slugs, birds and whatever else wants to nibble away at your food.

Getting to know your plants

The thing about patio growing is that you notice your plants more and pick out their peculiarities. Plants like to grow to certain heights, depending on their surroundings. So if you have cabbages raised off the ground, you will find they grow to a similar height than those in pots a few feet lower. This almost magical phenomenon is caused by the characteristics of the light in your garden. A row of cabbages in the ground never show this effect.

Take advantage of the shelter patios afford

Generally speaking, patios are warmer places than the open field. There is a number of elements to this. Firstly, your building itself can afford some shelter from driving wind and rain. Sunshine falling on the brickwork, as well as the patio floor, causes the building to warm up even in the coldest winters. This heat is released in the evening to keep the patio area a degree or two warmer and also reduces the length of time plants are exposed to the coldest temperatures.

Secondly, plants grown against or near walls often do better than those in the field or garden. The downside to this is that the property can shelter the patio from the sun. There is frequently nothing to be done about this, you can't move your house, but you can do something to mitigate the problem. You might be able to move your patio to a sunnier spot. If your garden is long, the patio might be best afforded at the end, if this part gets the most sun. There are no rules to say the patio must be next to the house. You can make a vertical patio ie, use a wall, be it a fence or the side of your house to grow on by using a series of hanging baskets and planters. Another solution to this problem is to raise your plants off the ground. If you find how your shadow falls it may be possible to raise them a little to bring them into the sunlight for longer.

Plastic fantastic

Another boon for the patio is the use of plastic. For very little money you can buy small plastic greenhouses that look more like wardrobes. Fix them to the house wall (because they are otherwise apt to blow away) and not only do they take up little space, the house should keep them frost-free for most of the year. A single tea light inside a hollow concrete breeze block, placed inside is enough for those really cold nights.

The Big Chill

That said, plants in pots suffer from the cold more than soil-borne ones. It takes a lot to freeze the soil down to a depth of 30cm, but a plant pot has roots in it only a few centimetres from the freezing air, and in the winter you will need to protect them. Bubble wrap is excellent for this, but so are newspapers and old woollies. Cover your plants with fleece or, better still, move them to a warmer spot. Lifting them from the ground is a good idea because cold air is heavier than warm and you can save a plant by simply putting it on a shelf.

Choosing your pots

The choice of pot is important. Clay pots tend to crack in the winter if there is a lot of moist compost inside it. Ice expands when it freezes, cracking the pot. Plastic pots are more able to withstand this kind of tension, but are less insulating than clay ones. Try planting in plastic, then putting this into a larger clay pot filled with stones or plastic packing to take up the space.

Fill a wheelbarrow (if you have space for one) or modify a shopping trolley to hold delicate plants so you can move them inside or into a warm spot for the night more easily and then drag them back into the light during the day.

FINDING NOVEL PLACES TO PLANT CROPS

Walls are there for more than hanging baskets. You can buy or make a wide range of plant holders that hang off the wall and in which you can grow food. Old plastic shoe racks, multi slotted and designed for hanging in wardrobes, also hang easily against the wall. I have used them to grow strawberries as well as all manner of herbs. If you drill and plug good quality coat hangers on the wall you can use them to site shopping bags that carry any amount of crops. For example, if you half fill a carrier bag with compost and grow a potato tuber in it, slightly closing off the neck when the vine has come out of the top of the bag, you can place this on a hook, watering with fertiliser solution. It works better if you put a black plastic bag over the shopping bag to stop the young potatoes from greening. You only get a small crop, perhaps only enough for a single meal. You can get carried away designing places to hang bags of growing potatoes – and you need only 180 of them for a year's supply – implausible but tempting!

Up on the roof

Roofs are excellent places to grow, but keep it lightweight, such as salad crops, garlic in pots and radish. Similarly, car ports are excellent places for growing crops, especially if you fit a plastic roof. A large tub with a vine trained along the car port makes a wonderful feature as well as several gallons of wine.

We have already mentioned the idea of lining paths with grow bags, and steps are a good place to place pots if it can be done safely. Similarly, the tops of walls and fences make for good growing places as long as they are safe to use. You can dangle bags on either side of a fence for growing on the top if you have access to either side, or a good neighbour.

Drainpipes

A completely fantastic way of growing crops is in drainpipes, which can be cut to size and then split into two length-ways. Tape the two halves back together (for ease of opening later) and block off the gap at the bottom. Fill with compost and grow carrots down the tube, and turnips, parsnips, herbs of all kinds, strawberries – almost anything. For root crops you can, when they're ready, break open the pipe again to reveal the most perfect crop ever.

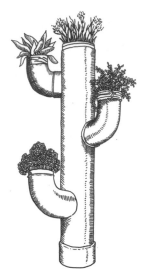

Fig. 2. Drainpipe herbs

Soil pipes

The thing about soil pipes is they are interconnecting. You can buy jointing bends which slot into each other and therefore make a tree in which will grow all kinds of crops. There is no end to the ways you can put them together. This type of container will fix to a wall very easily and make a back door herb garden, an interesting strawberry container, or salad container. It will fill with a huge amount of compost making it capable of growing some quite impressive crops.

Use, re-use, recycle . . .

You can re-use old lampshades by lining them with a plastic bag, filling them with compost and hanging them like baskets around the garden. Or why not try cutting the polystyrene packaging you get around televisions and white goods into receptacle shapes. You can use children's swimming pools and cleaned-out tin cans, plastic bottles, trays and dishes, mugs and cups (with drainage holes drilled in the bottom).

Old milk bottles – you can hardly call those plastic containers 'milk bottles' but they make excellent carrot growing containers. Fill the bottle with compost by three quarters and drop a couple of seeds into the bottle and water it. The bottle itself acts as a little greenhouse, the seeds grow up and eventually you can reject the poorest growing. After a while the plant grows through the hole in the top, and you have a carrot plant. You can do the same with many other root crops, or try starting off larger crops before transferring into a larger pot.

Everything including the kitchen sink

It might be amusing but many household items are good for growing. The kitchen sink, as well as making a great pond, is good for growing herbs and if you keep the drainer you have a surface for pots too. Try to get some plants growing out of the taps! It's harder than you think.

Toilets and potties are traditionally used with a wry smile in the garden, but ensure you give them a thorough cleaning before you grow crops in them. Still, I think they are better for growing flowers.

Refrigerators have excellent uses in the garden. You can remove the door and use the space as a cold frame, especially if you have a piece of clear plastic to cover it. They can also be used to grow mushrooms inside, because they are easy to clean, insulated and dark when you close the door.

IT'S A WHAT?

In some circumstances, especially when you are growing cabbages and their related crops in pots, what you end up with bears no visible relationship to what you would buy in the shop. A recognisable, round-hearted cabbage is turned into a 2m tall, long leaved plant. Cabbages show what botanists call polymorphism; that is they adopt one shape in the garden and a completely different shape in a pot. This phenomenon is quite common, though less marked in other crops than with cabbages. Saying that, the cabbages you get in a pot still have a lot of cabbage leaf on them. They might not look like cabbage leaves, but they certainly taste like them. If you plant an onion set into a piece of compost-filled drainpipe, it will grow quite happily, but not achieve the same size as its soil-grown sibling. But it's still an onion, and there is nothing to stop you from growing hundreds of them along paths, against walls, on shed roofs and so on.

JUST HOW MUCH CAN YOU GROW?

The simple answer, of course, depends on how much space you have. We have already seen some ways for getting more crops in and I am sure you can use your imagination to find even more. The point of patio growing is improving your life. How lovely to have a row of salad onions to brighten up your summer salads! Even better to have a year's supply of lettuces, or turnips that were growing one minute, roasting the next! Then, best of all, a week's worth of potatoes for every month between July and December. You might not be self sufficient, but you can be well on the way, and if all the space you have is a landing on the north face of a high rise block of flats, you can still take great pride in the meagre crop you can grow there.

And in all vegetable growing, pride is the best seasoning of all.

Window boxes

You can increase your growing area considerably by making use of securely fixed window boxes. It is possible to obtain a week's worth of crops from a window box and as much as a month's supply from them around the whole house. You can get a continual supply of cut-and-come-again herbs and salad crops. More than mere window boxes, you can affix boxes directly to walls for the same effect. I like to place a bracket on the wall that allows me to hang the boxes and remove them once they are used. This way I can leave the wall free and rotate the boxes or stack them as I require.

It is possible to fix cloches to window boxes as long as you are sure it is secure. A cloche is a transparent covering for growing plants, keeping them warm and protecting them from the wind. The thought of scratching a neighbour's car because the wind has blown the cover and/or the box itself down the street, is enough to keep me awake all night.

Window growing

Growing on the outside of the window can be matched by growing on the inside of the window. The kitchen windowsill is probably the very first place a child begins growing food. There are very few people who haven't, as a child, grown cress in an eggshell or carrot tops in a saucer. Windowsills can maintain even temperatures and good light intensities, so it makes sense to use them. It is an easy job to put some shelving up at the windowsill, especially in an infrequently-used room. This is the ideal spot for starting seedlings, especially as the trays do not take up all of the space and block off lots of light.

Make a frame

Many of you will know the A-frames standing outside shops. If you put a couple of supporting 'legs' on the open side of a pallet, you get a directional A-frame fence against which you can grow all kinds of crops, particularly courgettes or cucumbers. You can even build a container at the bottom of the pallet for the plant to grow in.

CHAPTER 2

PLANNING FOR CROPS ALL THE YEAR ROUND

John Milton in *Paradise Lost* tells us that before God constructed the universe, he made a plan. A plan is the most useful tool in the gardener's armoury because without it we end up with a confused garden, and even if we come to dislike our plan, we can always make ourselves another.

WHAT TOOLS DO I NEED?

You don't need many tools for patio gardening. By far the most important thing is to have a space where you can fill plant pots and containers with compost, and maybe a riddle (a wire mesh sieve) to filter the compost through. You will also need a supply of clear polythene bags to fit over plant pots and an endless supply of elastic bands to hold them in place.

Watering cans

You will need four watering cans.

Two ordinary watering cans with fine roses are needed, one for general watering or feeding and one if you are going to use insecticide. In addition to this, a foliar spray for leafy plants is useful and another fine spray bottle if you are going to use any chemicals to get rid of aphids etc. It is useful to have an outdoor source to fill them from; it's always a problem having to walk with dirty feet into the kitchen. An outdoor tap is a boon, as is a suitably protected water butt. I say protected because the thought of a child climbing into it is horrific.

Irrigation systems

It is easier to incorporate automatic irrigation systems on the patio than to the rest of the garden. You can buy the appropriate step down tubing from garden centres or online from any polytunnel suppliers. Once you have your tubing from the tap to the narrow gauge plastic, you can easily improvise by attaching plastic tubing from tropical fish suppliers. The systems work either from a manifold, with lots of tubes feeding a few containers, or a single tube that has little holes in it which you lay over the pots. You can pierce the tubing at the appropriate point.

Overhead irrigation systems consist of a spray nozzle which wets a whole area as though it was raining.

A much simpler way of irrigating a number of pots at the same time is to place them on wet, absorbent material. The cheapest way is a tray filled with compost upon which you stand ceramic pots, which draw up water by capillary action. You can buy special dripping irrigation systems that flow water onto an absorbent mat. I have found a sufficiently effective alternative is made using a large (four litres if you can get it) lemonade bottle filled with water and placed either onto the absorbent mat or directly in the container itself. The bottle is pierced with a single small hole and the flow can be controlled by leaving the lid on tight or undoing it a little.

Spades, forks, rakes and things

If your gardening involves growing in pots and containers, you won't need any tools. The largest implement you will need is a garden trowel, and since you do not have to spend a fortune on larger equipment, you might as well buy the best you can afford. Good tools are a pleasure to use and will last forever. Buy trowels that have a leather lanyard attached to the end so you can tie it around your wrist when in use. I have learned from experience that it is one thing leaving a tool in a large bed, where it is always visible; quite another to leave it amongst some pots, where it can remain hidden for months. Other 'digging' duties can be satisfactorily achieved by using spoons. A table spoon for loosening compost, a dessert spoon for adding fertiliser and a tea spoon for uprooting plants.

An old dining fork is ideal for manipulating compost in seed trays as well as opening bottles and the very best tool for transplanting seedlings is an old pencil.

Cutting

Perhaps the most sophisticated garden equipment you will need is a good pair of secateurs. A pair of scissors will do for many things, but eventually you need to cut through wood, and only secateurs will do. A penknife is good for many tasks, especially grafting buds and cutting string, and when (or if) it becomes necessary to cut large branches, a small tenon saw will suffice.

Storage

Somewhere to put utensils is more important than having them in the first place. Even a patio gardener needs storage space, and you can buy or make waterproof, lockable boxes if you haven't room for a shed. You can redeem the space taken up by your store by putting pots on top of it. Plants or compost heaps are ideal ways to hide tools. I have once kept my garden tools in a special plastic box hidden in a pile of horse manure and no one ever dreamed of plunging their hand inside to get at them. If only they knew how!

Fig. 3. Secateurs

Caring for tools

Make sure your tools are always in good condition. This means having somewhere secure to put them when not in use, but more importantly keeping them clean and storing them correctly. Remove dirt from trowels and then plunge them into a trowel safe three or four times after use. This is a box or bucket of sand laden with a litre of ordinary oil, sunflower or vegetable is fine. The action of plunging into the sand keeps the edges clean and the oil makes sure the blade is protected from the atmosphere.

Have a jar of disinfectant ready to clean cutting tools. If you are pruning around the garden make sure you wipe the blades with disinfectant between cuts, like a surgeon stopping infection between plants. Always put your tools away clean and disinfected. Make it a habit and it will become a regular part of the gardening routine, a kind of Zen.

TRAYS AND PROPAGATORS

Late winter to early spring is always a busy time for starting off seeds. By far the easiest way to begin is to have plenty of trays available and somewhere warm for them to germinate and grow. Propagators are useful if you have a couple of trays to get going, but they take up so much room. I have found it much easier to use a warm, light-filled room. A dining table next to a window works just as well. Seed trays can be made from old plates or modified cat litter trays, or simply buy the purpose-made ones from the garden centre. You can buy module trays which have individual compartments for seeds to be planted in, making it easier to transplant the seedling. However, they are likely to be constructed from thin plastic which means they can be used only once.

I have to say that building individual pots out of newspaper has long been my favourite activity on a rainy day, and you can buy a special wooden tool that makes the job a pleasure. Alternatively, use a strip of newspaper roughly 15cm long and a plastic cup, roll the newspaper around the sides until three or four sheets thick and fold the base under. Remove the inside cup and fill the paper pot with compost. Pots made from recycled paper can be easily planted into larger pots intact. The paper rots in the pot gradually to release the roots. You can help this process on its way using a penknife, just tearing the paper a little.

PROVIDING A CONSTANT ENVIRONMENT FOR SEEDS

When seedlings appear, either in trays or modules or your homemade paper pots, they need consistent conditions. Your first imperative is to get the seed wet at a temperature of around 12°C or above. You should look on your seed packet for specific requirements. Once germination has been achieved, keep the seedlings in a constant environment. It doesn't really matter if the temperature is a little lower than that needed for germination, just keep the seeds from draughts and cold water. In order to do this properly you need to plan the space you are going to use. It takes up to a month to grow seedlings ready for transplantation and you will need to put them somewhere. Of course many crops can be started at other times of the year, but between the months of January and March you need to provide a reasonably warm, draught-free growing space for all those seedlings.

PLANNING CROPS

Although there are some exceptions, it is possible to grow more or less anything from the greengrocers on a patio of one sort or another. Some plants, such as asparagus, need special care and continual attention to their roots. However, asparagus can be grown in a dustbin but it needs new compost and careful removal of spent compost in the early spring. Growing this plant in a dustbin offers a neat solution to the amount of land it needs. Further, you can put on the lid in the winter for added protection. Incidentally, the same goes for crops like rhubarb, where you can use the dustbin lid to blanch the stalks.

The list that follows is a general planting/timing guide and will apply equally to plants destined for more conventional gardens. In Chapter 5 we will look at the specific requirements for individual crops.

Crop	Sowing	Growing	Maintenance	Pests
Asparagus	Sow and plant in March/April	Grow for three years before taking crop in May/June	Keep richly fed and don't let it dry out completely	
Aubergine	Sow in March at 20°C	Transplant until they are in 30cm pots in the greenhouse	Keep well fed during growing season, feed weekly. Harvest when full coloured.	Aphids mostly, though can get fungal infections
Basil	Sow in March in cool greenhouse	Transplant to growing spot in late April	Keep well fed and watered. Ideal pot plant.	Aphids
Beans (broad)	Sow in pots in cool greenhouse from October onwards	Transplant to growing pot either in November or early spring	Keep weed-free and well fed – a good mulch of compost is useful	Blackfly mostly and viral infections
Beans (French and runner)	Sow in growing position in April with supporting canes	Train the plants around a wigwam. Keep well fed and watered.	The best flavour comes from well watered plants dosed with liquid feed. Harvest regularly for more crop.	Aphids, birds, mice

Beetroot	Sow in late March under cover and outdoors after April right through to summer	Thin to about 15cm and keep weed-free.	Don't let them dry completely and feed with a little well-rotted manure or liquid feed once a month. Harvest as you like them – from leaves to cricket ball sized roots.	
Broccoli	Sow indoors in pots from December. Sow outdoors in March/April.	Transfer to 45cm rows in April/May. Firm well in.	Soil should be well dug and the plants should be firmed in regularly. Harvest when the heads are formed and tight.	
Cabbage (summer)	Sow in pots in cool greenhouse in March	Transplant to growing positions in late April	Keep weed-free at 45cm apart. Harvest when ready in early- to mid-summer.	White fly, aphids, insects
Cabbage (autumn)	Sow in pots in a cool greenhouse in April and transplant in late May	Grow at 60cm apart for large balls, keep weed-free and mulch with good compost	Water evenly, do not let them dry out or they will split on watering	White fly, aphids, insects
Calabrese	Sow in spring for a summer harvest or late September, indoors for a spring harvest	Spring-sown plants should be grown to 45cm. Autumn plants in pots and transplanted in late October.	Reasonably fertile is important. Make sure plants are firm in the ground.	White fly
Carrot	Sow thinly under cloches in March or directly into the ground from April to July. Sow also in September under cloches.	Thin out to about 15cm apart. Harvest from the end of May onwards and in the early spring if sown in autumn.	Well-worked sandy soil with lots of nutrients	Protect from carrot root fly and cover with fleece in the coldest months

Cauliflower	Sow in December under heat and transplant in April, or in pots indoors in March, or May for winter types	Transplant to growing positions 45cm apart when plants are 8cm tall. Add lime to the holes.	Harvest when headed up properly. You should have a good supply of cauliflowers all the year round. Make sure they are firmly placed.	Clubroot, whitefly and aphids as well as other insects
Celeriac	Sow in March/April under heat and transplant in May	Keep watered and well fed. This plant takes a long time to reach maturity.	Harvest from October until late winter	
Celery	Sow at room temperature in March	Transplant to a deep trench of well-rotted manure in May	This plant is very hungry. Keep weed-free and in the summer water with some liquid feed. Blanch by drawing compost up the stems	Aphids and viral diseases
Chicory	Sow indoors in pots or modules in April or outside in May. You can also sow in August.	Transplant or thin out in May. Grow at 45cm apart.	Harvest as the plant stems and roots swell	Aphids mostly
Chillies	Almost like tomatoes, sow in March/April in the greenhouse	Transplant when handleable to small pots and thence to larger ones until in 30cm pots	Harvest when the fruits are ripe in late summer. Can be grown in grow bags. Water and feed regularly.	Aphids, fungal infections and red spider mite
Courgette	Sow in pots indoors in April and transplant in May. You can also sow in June outside.	Transplant pot-grown types in June onto a mound of richly fed and well dug ground	Water well at the base and feed regularly. Try not to wet the leaves too much. Watch the humidity. Harvest as the courgettes appear.	Fungal infections and aphids
Cucumber	Sow indoors in March in pots or outdoors in June	Transplant to growing position in June. Soil to be well dug	Water and feed well. Provide protection against cold and wet weather	

Endive	Sow in May/June in growing position	Provide plenty of water and feed regularly. Blanch leaves with plant pot.	Some say sow indoors in pots in April. Endives are troublesome to transplant.	Aphids
Fennel	Sow indoors in March under heat or outdoors in June	Transplant in June. Needs good rich soil – well drained.	Feed once a month. Harvest when bases are full.	
Garlic	Plant in good rich soil from October onwards	Feed well for the best flavour and do not protect from frost	Keep weed-free and harvest in late summer onwards	
Jerusalem artichoke	Plant from March until May	Leave all the year in ground at 45cm apart	Harvest in the following January	
Kale	Sow in sequentially from April until May	Thin out to about 45cm and keep well fed and weed-free	Harvest at the end of summer and through autumn and winter. You can keep a supply going all year.	
Leek	Sow from December to March under heat	Transplant to final growing holes by April/May	Keep well fed. Cut a hole and simply position plant in place. Some top and tail them. Don't let them dry out, feed monthly. Harvest when needed.	
Lettuce	Sow indoors in winter and outdoors from spring right through to summer	They need up to 12 weeks to grow, so you can have lettuce all year round	They do not transplant well after being a few centimetres tall, best grown in situ. Space to around 30–45cm.	Aphids and pigeons

Onions	Sow indoors in December	Plant sets in March/April or in October	Plant continuously and have a longer harvest over a couple of months. Harvest in late summer and store carefully.	Aphids and fungal infections
Parsley	Sow outdoors from April until July	Keep well fed and do not let it dry too much	Sow regularly for tender leaves	
Parsnip	Sow in March/April in drills outdoors	Thin to 40cm and feed regularly over the summer	Keep weed-free in soil that is finely chopped as for carrots. Harvest in December/January.	Carrot root fly, canker
Peas	Can sow indoors in September, mostly outdoors from March/April to June	Transplant into growing positions when 5cm. Provide support and keep in fairly rich soil. Don't let them dry completely	Harvest when the pods are full	Aphids, slugs, mice, birds
Potatoes	Plant early potatoes in March, and main crop in April	Plant at 45cm apart in well-dug, very rich soil. Don't let them dry, earth up.	Harvest early potatoes in July/August, maincrop in August/September	Aphids, blight
Radish	Sow from March under cloche then from late April outdoors until July	Keep weed-free, thin to about 20cm and feed fortnightly	Harvest from early summer onwards. Grow indoors from November for a winter crop.	
Rhubarb	Plant crowns in Jan/March in very rich, well-rotted manure and compost	Keep watered and fed all the first year. Remove stalks in October as they die.	Harvest the following May/June. Take only the young leaves. A hungry plant.	Aphids and some viral infections

Shallots	Sow indoors in December	Plant sets in March/April or in October	Harvest in late summer store carefully, make pickles	Aphids and fungal infections
Spinach	Sow indoors from December and outdoors from March	Don't over feed – it accumulates nitrates	Thin to about 30cm, keep weed-free	
Swede	Sow in April/May – protect from frost	Thin to 45cm and keep weed-free. Feed once a month if you can.	Harvest from September	Clubroot
Sweetcorn	Sow indoors in April, two seeds per pot	Plant out in May in a square grid for pollination	Rich soil is good, keep warm – protect from windy rain. Harvest when seeds are just juicy	
Tomato	Sow in March in pots indoors	Transplant sequentially in pots until plant is 20cm. Water evenly – never allow to dry.	Grow in grow bags, water and feed weekly in summer. Harvest when red! (Or orange, yellow, or as a last resort – green.)	Aphids, fungal and viral problems, blight
Turnip	Sow in rows from March until July	Thin to 30cm. Feed and water well.	Harvest when cricket ball size from August onwards	

GROWING FRUIT

Though the most common idea of an orchard is a vast patch of land, it is still possible to get a lot of fruit into a small space and you are not restricted to the kinds of fruit you can grow. In a way, the highest technical achievements can be gained from growing fruit on the patio. For example, an excellent growing method for apples is to espalier them along a wire framework against a wall. This is a method of pruning and training the branches of a fruit tree to grow in a single plane and is extremely popular in the large walled gardens of stately homes. The same is true for all top fruit.

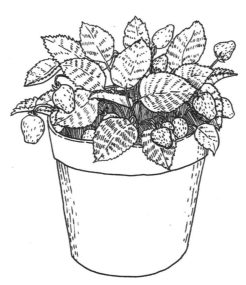

Fig. 4. Strawberry pot

The following table applies to fruit destined for all kinds of growing situations, not just the patio and we shall come back to them in later chapters for specific guidance.

Crop	Sowing	Growing	Maintenance	Pests
Apple	Plant into container in winter	Grow for three years before taking crop	Dwarf forms need little care save extra rotted manure/compost in spring. Feed regularly in summer.	Aphids and fungal infections
Apricot	Plant into container in winter	Possibly best under cover or against a southerly facing wall	Needs to be kept warm, well pruned and well fed	
Blackcurrant	Plant in November	Need to be pruned and fed in spring	Keep feeding during growing period	

Currants (other)	Plant in November	Need to be pruned and fed in spring	Keep feeding during growing period	
Fig	Plant into container in winter	Feed in spring and keep richly fed	Fruits stay on the plant a long time	
Gooseberries	Plant in February	Feed in spring and keep watered at base	Prune to an open aspect, collect fruit in summer	
Grapes	Plant in late winter/early spring	Feed well-rotted manure and liquid feed. Can grow indoors or out.	Complex pruning, but plenty of grapes	Fungal infections
Kiwi	Plant in spring	Feed with liquid feed and fresh compost	Prune in April	
Peach	Plant into container in winter	Feed in spring and summer. Keep frost-free.	Don't over water: allow the compost to dry out before watering	Leaf curl
Pear	Plant into container in winter	Grow for three years before taking crop	Dwarf forms need little care save extra rotted manure/compost in spring. Feed regularly in summer.	Aphids and fungal infections
Plum	Plant into container in winter	Grow for three years before taking crop	Add extra rotted manure/compost in spring. Feed regularly in summer.	Aphids and fungal infections
Rhubarb	Plant in January	Blanch until needed in spring	Feed heavily in late spring and early winter	
Strawberry	Plant in spring	Propagate the plants from runners	Feed during the summer in containers, employ a three-year rotation	

CHAPTER 3

PLANTS GROW DIFFERENTLY IN POTS

It is true to say that you can grow anything in a pot that you would normally grow in the garden. I would go further than this and say that you can grow enough of any crop plant, vegetable or fruit to make its care worthwhile. However, in some cases there is at least one proviso.

We have to remember that plants take up a lot of invisible space. Normally a healthy plant will have a root system as large beneath the ground as the rest of the plant above. If the patio is restricted anywhere it is here, beneath the ground. By growing in pots we restrict the plant at the root level, and this has consequences.

WHAT DO PLANTS NEED?

Oxygen and carbon dioxide

All plants need air from which their supply of oxygen and carbon dioxide is taken. Whereas it is true that leaves produce oxygen as a by-product of photosynthesis, this doesn't mean the plant can survive without adequate oxygen. There is no efficient way of pumping oxygen around a plant and so if roots become waterlogged, or for some reason the soil in the roots becomes stagnant, they can die from oxygen starvation. Compost in pots should always be fluffy and full of air, though it is correct practice to compact plants into their pots. The compost will spring out to reveal air spaces anyway.

You can increase the available air spaces in a pot of compost by adding grit, sand or a material called pearlite, which is made from mica. However, if you are growing crops such as carrots, you will find the presence of grit will make the roots grow into strange shapes.

Water

There is an inverse relationship between air spaces and dampness of soil. Sand has a lot of air, not much water. Clay holds a lot of water but has no air at all. The pot of compost has to provide a balance of both. Interestingly, sand has no air available to the plant either because the root gets its oxygen from that dissolved in the tiny film of water that surrounds the soil particles.

The problem with pots and containers is they are too free draining, and consequently most plants on patios need watering daily in the summertime, even if it is raining.

WATER TEMPERATURE

If you were to have a cold shower in the height of the day you would complain, and so do growing plants. Cold water can bring the metabolism of the plant to a standstill and continued dousing makes it produce woody tissue, making the vegetable somewhat tougher. The best way of watering is to have a reservoir of water that has had a chance to warm up before taking it away to the plants. Secondly, try to water at the base of the plants.

WHEN SHOULD YOU WATER?

There has been a lot of talk over the years about scorching the plants by watering them at the height of the day. Small beads of water act like a lens, magnifying the sun's rays and scorching the leaf on which it stands. On the patio there is more to think about. Pots and containers lose water quickly and their inhabitants are more likely to wilt. This is a desperate situation for the plant and in order to add support, the plant produces more woody tissue. Do not be afraid of watering at the height of the day. It is good to avoid splashing the leaves if possible, but remember plants cannot draw water from beyond the boundaries of the pot, so provide water when it is needed.

WHEN A PLANT WILTS

Plants are amazing. They are held upright by water tension, columns of water in reinforced tubes that give the plant strength. When there is no water about, the roots cannot replace the water lost in the leaves and eventually the columns inside the plants break under the stress. When this happens the column is filled with air and cannot be replaced. If you sit in a field on a hot day you can hear some of these columns popping under the stress of drought. If you continually allow your plants to wilt before watering

Fig. 5. Wilting plant

29

they will eventually become sick as fungi takes advantage of the broken tissues in the stem.

WHICH PLANTS ARE PRONE TO WILTING?

Water is lost to the atmosphere by evaporation from the leaves. Consequently plants with large leaves will transpire, or take water from the roots and up through the plant, more rapidly than plants with smaller ones. Plants with waxy leaves will transpire even less. Lettuces, turnips and most brassicas amaze as to how quickly they can dry a plant pot. Carrots and plants with hairy leaves use much less water. In the heat of an August day you can water lettuces two or three times if they are growing in a pot. I have found that a drip system, with water, with fertiliser dissolved in it, provides excellent conditions for salad growth. It needn't be an expensive one either – simply a plastic bottle with a pin prick will suffice, placed on top of a container of salad plants.

Plants need all kinds of mineral nutrients

Even in the soil of the garden, plants use up a lot of nutrients and the soil becomes less productive. If you were to take a plant, roots and all, and burn it until there was nothing left but ash, this would give you some comparative idea of the amount of nutrients removed from the soil. At the level of the plant pot and container, the mineral nutrients in the growing medium are soon removed. They are either taken up by the plant or washed away by the watering regime. Consequently, plants growing in containers need a constant flow of nutrients.

The most convenient, and possibly the most expensive, way to keep the nutrient level high is to put slow release fertiliser pellets into the compost. As the pellets are wetted a little of them dissolves into the compost and this then feeds the plants. A regime of feeding when watering is another idea, but you have to be sure the feed is not too strong.

HOMEMADE FERTILISERS

An organic method is to stuff a pillow case with cow manure and allow this to soak in a 204 litre barrel of water. Dilute this by half with clean water. An alternative is to stuff the pillow case with comfrey leaves and make a tea in exactly the same way. It is a good idea to renew the leaves monthly, though it's a really smelly job.

A WORD ABOUT GREEN FERTILISERS

A lot of people grow green manures for use in the greenhouse and around the garden. They do work, but they take a little thinking about. You grow a crop in the ground for its mineral content, but where have those minerals come from? Of course they have come from the soil the plant is growing in. For a good supply of 'green manure' you need to feed the plants you will harvest as fertiliser.

RICH COMPOST

People who garden in small areas have little room for compost heaps and what space they do have is taken up by the ubiquitous green council bin. The total output of these bins is very low, not really enough over the year to provide all you need. A way round this is to buy a kitchen composter. These little bins take all food – even meat. You cover the waste with an activated bran, which digests everything and provides a rich liquid that can be used in your watering. The solid waste can then be transferred to the compost bin.

Keep your compost bin warm! Wrap it in bubble wrap and when the compost is ready, mix it with the cheapest bought stuff you can find. Often you can get a good deal in October on unsold growbags. They are frequently available at less than half price. Enrich this cheap compost with the rich stuff you have made yourself.

MANY PLANTS NEED SYMBIOTIC FUNGI

Most plants, especially the brassica family (cabbages, sprouts, broccoli etc.) will not grow too well in sterile conditions. The reason for this is that naturally they have a little help from a fungus that grows through the roots and ramificates through the whole plant. This plant/fungus interaction is one where both organisms benefit. In particular, the plant benefits from the fungal ability to release from the soil nutrients the plant cannot access.

Normally the fungi are resident in soil and whereas plants will grow where the fungi are not present, many of them do so much better when their symbiotic partners are present. In order to improve the chances of the symbiotic relationship, add some soil to your compost.

TYPES OF COMPOST

Most people either buy or make compost. The whole world of composting is slightly confusing, and is often undertaken as though it were some form of 'dark art' or gardening witchcraft. The simple truth is that if you pile up plant material it will rot down until the plants and animals living off the rotting material can get no more goodness from it. What is left can be thrown back on the garden to give minerals and structure back to the earth.

There are all kinds of composts out there; some for growing seeds, others for mature plants, and if you make your own, you need to be sure it has completely finished rotting down. You do this by doing the nose test – have a good smell, and it if smells sweet and earthy, you are ready. You have to use your eyes too – it should look dark and crumbly.

John Innes soil-based compost

Three types of compost were designed by the John Innes Institute, for starting seeds off, followed by 'potting them on' to their next stage and finally growing mature plants. They were John Innes 1, 2 and 3, and the system was designed to go from No 1 to No 3. Most gardeners don't bother with the system any more, but it is very useful for patio gardeners. I strongly believe it is time to revive its use because since the compost is soil based, and packed with nutrients, it doesn't rot in the pots. Sometimes you buy compost, particularly organic compost, and it is still rotting down in the bag so when you use it your plants rot too!

A WORD ABOUT ORGANIC GROWING AND THE PATIO

Organic gardening is the way people should go these days, but there is an enormous **but**.

For patio growers, you don't have to look after the soil as much as you do in the rest of the garden. What does it matter if you add superphosphate to your compost? You are not changing the soil, just the little amount in your pot. Organic gardening principles should be adhered to when it comes to insecticides and dangerous chemicals, but there is nothing wrong with adding a touch of packet fertiliser to the pots.

THE PATIO VERSION OF JOHN INNES COMPOST
Use this as multi-purpose compost in all your pots and containers.

To make your own John Innes compost, first mix 7 parts of loam (good quality soil), 3 of peat substitute and then 2 of sand.

Add per 1 cubic metre of mix of:

   0.5kg ground limestone
   1kg general all purpose fertiliser

SUPPORT

One of the functions of roots is to hold the plant securely in the soil. This hardly ever happens properly in a pot or container. Once the roots touch the side of the pot they start to grow in a strange way, some distort, some roots stop growing altogether. Consequently, pot- and container-grown plants are frequently short of support. You might find yourself needing to support the most unlikely of plants, London lettuces being the most pathetic I have ever tried. There is no hard-and-fast rule as to which plants need support, and the best thing to do is to keep an eye on things as they grow.

Brussels sprouts

It is a curious thing that sprouts prefer to be in soil that is well firmed in. If they grow in a loose soil the sprout buds do not form evenly and appear to explode. This being the case, I make a point of going round firming them at the roots when grown in largish containers. I also support the stems strongly to keep them from falling over. I have tried many ways of doing this. Firstly, I tried growing them in large oblong tubs against a wall, with the individual plants tied to it. This worked quite well. I also tried staking them in individual 30cm pots, which didn't do so well.

Some plants change shape

If you grow a cabbage in an ordinary garden bed it will grow into a ball-shaped cabbage, just as you expect. If, however, you grow a cabbage in a plant pot you are much more likely to see it 'run to seed'. This is a phenomenon where the plant responds to its environment and provides us with something of a surprise. In the case of a cabbage the plant grows about 2m tall and is covered with much smaller leaves. That said, if you take all the leaves from the elongated cabbage and weigh them you will find that the yield is much the same as the cabbage growing in the ground.

The cabbage leaves, though different in shape and slightly different in texture, are just as good to eat. In some cases, you need to get used to seeing your produce in a slightly different light. Instead of being a round ball, the cabbage becomes a plant that can be used as a cut-and-come-again!

Small is beautiful

Another major difference with some container-grown plants is yield. Constricted roots do not always work as well as they should. When they touch the side of the container some plants change their metabolism and slow down vegetative growth in favour of flower production. This can be valuable in the case of peas, but not so if you are trying to grow turnips.

Another factor is the mass of nutrients needed to make a mature plant. It is hardly possible in some growing situations to provide enough. You simply cannot make a cubic foot of compost provide enough minerals if the plant has evolved to live in 10 cubic metres. The plant produces a smaller version of itself. But this doesn't mean that the produce is not worth growing. It might be small, but as they say, it is perfectly formed!

FLAVOUR

If a plant has a strong flavour it usually takes a lot of chemicals to actually make it. For example, onions and garlic have a strong flavour, as we all know. This comes from a number of complex molecules containing sulphur. In order to create them the plant does some complex chemistry that converts sulphates to sulphites and sulphides, which are then incorporated into a protein. It is the sulphates in the soil that are needed for good onion and garlic flavour. Similarly, carrots and parsnips need a good supply of magnesium. To make sure the produce you grow is full of flavour, pack the compost with balanced fertiliser. If all you do is fill a pot with compost and then water the plant until you eat it, don't expect it to be fully flavoured, or fully formed for that matter.

SKIN

Plants grown in a conventional way are insulated by the soil they grow in. In these conditions the plant provides itself with a protective skin usually in proportion to the variation in temperature. In a pot or container, the plant experiences a wider range of temperatures and this fluctuation can create a thicker skin, especially in plants like turnips. To get round this, feed and water regularly and insulate your pots.

COMPANION PLANTING

Over time, nature crams the greatest variety of plants into the smallest area it can. We tend to do the opposite, with beds, and even whole fields, filled with just one type of plant. This is a situation asking for trouble. If the only thing beneath a flying insect is a plot full of cabbages, it's likely to land on a cabbage. However, if there is a variety of colours and crops in your plot, there's a much greater chance that the insect will land on something other than your precious food plant and it will probably fly a little further to where there are easier pickings. This is the simple premise for having a great diversity of plants and crops in the garden, and especially on the patio.

One plant per pot

Most of the time we grow a single plant in a pot on the patio, partly because there is not so much room for the roots of two or more incumbents. However, there are good reasons for companion planting, that is growing a number of plants together, if you have the space.

There are many combinations of plants that are beneficial, but there are a few that aren't recommended, for various reasons. Garlic, for example, may taint the flavour of peas, beans and cabbages.

There are many interactions between plants in the soil that we don't fully understand. In some cases beneficial fungi are killed off by the fungi of the competing plant, in other cases chemicals from one plant inhibit the growth of another. In most cases, however, the presence of one plant actually enhances the growth of the other. The table below is a good guide for companion plants.

Main crop	Suggested companion	Best to avoid
Alliums (garlic, onions)	Carrots, turnips	Watch out for taint on beans
Brassicas (cabbage family)	Marigolds, rosemary	Onions
Beans	Almost anything	Onions, garlic
Carrot	Onions, peas	
Lettuce	Carrots, strawberries	
Peas	Almost anything	Onions, garlic
Potatoes	Marigolds, beans	Tomatoes (same family)
Strawberries	Beans, lettuce	All alliums
Tomatoes	Parsley, marigolds	Potatoes
Turnips, swede	Alliums, marigolds	

Companion planting in separate pots

When you assemble an array of different plants together, each in their separate pot, you miss out on any interaction at the root level, but this doesn't mean you cannot benefit from growing plants together.

We have already hinted that there is good reason to mix your pots so the plants copy nature. Let us say you have a cabbage in one pot surrounded by six smaller pots filled with marigolds. The marigolds look lovely and add variety to the garden, they distract insects from your crop and make it difficult for others too. Mice, birds and butterflies, aphids and whiteflies are all less likely to create a menace among your cabbage. The same goes for carrots which, if you surround with spring onions in pots, or garlic plants, will be less troubled by carrot root fly. Your plan should be to disguise all your planting by surrounding them with lots of others of different species.

Fig. 6. Cabbage and marigold

Top five companion plants

MARIGOLD

You should grow hundreds of marigolds. Apart from being pretty they draw insects to our plants, mostly beneficial ones. Modern research shows they put chemicals into the soil that protect their roots from chemical attack and these can benefit our crop plants too if we grow them in the same container. Finally, many animals, including slugs and snails, don't like the smell of marigold flowers, which drives them away – hopefully onto the neighbour's plot!

LAVENDER

The heady smell of lavender is as good for humans as it is for the garden. Tudor potagers were ringed with lavender. This attractive plant not only smells heavenly but also attracts hundreds of insects while also providing an antiseptic in the soil.

ONION

Onions, chives, and leeks go well with carrots and parsnips. Their aroma confuses the carrot fly and there is a 75% chance of the little insect going somewhere else. Make a circle of these alliums in planters and grow the carrots in the middle.

BASIL

This strongly smelling plant is enough to deter many insects and all but the most Mediterranean of slugs and snails. It complements most plants and is good on pizzas too!

RADISH

The evidence is that slugs just love radishes. The hot root is a magnet for slugs and they are such 'easy grow' plants you can sow a few seeds here and there to act as sacrificial slug feeders. They will eat the radishes before your crops. You can easily see where the culprits are too, and deal with them accordingly.

DON'T FORGET WILDLIFE

Look after nature and she will look after you. What would summer be like without cabbage white butterflies? What would the blue tits eat – or ladybirds and lacewings for that matter – if we cleared all our gardens of greenfly and blackfly? Nature's variety is important and on her systems we all depend, so it's important we do our bit to maintain them. Leave a corner and a few pots of crop plants for all those insects and so-called pests to keep a foothold on life. Even slugs have a place in organic gardens, albeit a small one.

CHAPTER 4

THE PATIO GARDENER'S YEAR

There are many jobs the patio gardener has to get through during the year, and whereas the timescales overlap and some of them are ongoing throughout the whole year, everything seems to have its season.

This chapter concentrates on the general jobs and tasks to be completed during the year. Chapter 5 looks at all the plants on our list in Chapter 2 in greater detail.

IN THE WINTER

This is the time I always take to clean everything, to buy, make, and repair containers and pots, and to make sure everything is ready for the onslaught of the spring. Growing in pots and containers is unusual because you miss out on nature's way of cleaning. For example, if a part of a plant dies in the soil somewhere in the garden, you can be almost certain that the bacteria and fungi that rotted it will have been eaten or somehow removed by some other living organism and there will be no need to sterilise the soil. However, if the same thing happens in a pot on the patio you can be certain that there are no cleaning organisms to remove the infection left in the pot. Unless you disinfect the pot, there will be a larger concentration of pathogens and rotting organisms, which do not bode well for a completely healthy plant next season.

Wash all your containers in hot soapy water and rinse them in a solution of a gardening disinfectant or Milton sterilising solution type material. If you live near an agricultural suppliers, buy some udder wash instead of disinfectant because it does the job just as well and is much cheaper. Similarly, wash all your utensils, shelves, greenhouse or equivalent – everything your plants come into contact with or are grown in. It is also a good idea to put your gardening gloves or any protective clothing you might use through the washing machine.

Having cleaned your tools, sharpen any blades and give them all a good covering of oil. You can use a sharpening service at some garden centres and the larger DIY outlets. It is a wonderful feeling to work with a tool in its best condition, even if it is old. When growing plants in pots and containers you do not need large tools, but secateurs, knives, snippers and trowels need to be sharp.

Check your compost

Winter days are also a good time to look at compost. Assuming all the space you have is a patio, you will not have enough room for an extensive range of composters. I always close up my composter in September and leave it until January. I have two composters side by side which are actually like wheelie bins with a little door at the bottom. One is full and the other is empty. In January I empty as much good compost from the bottom of the filled bin as I can and then transfer all the rest into the next bin, which I have left empty for that purpose. This action puts a good deal of air into the compost, but at the same time cools it a great deal. I now have an empty composter again and another which I fill up over the following weeks.

By midsummer the compost in the bin is ready for use and I transfer it to bags for storage leaving me with an empty bin and the other for filling with material. In January, I estimate how much compost I need for the following year and use the compost I have made to enrich whatever I have left over from pots or have bought as cheap grow bags, etc. Compost is cheap in January, so buying early, or last year's leftovers is a good idea.

COMPOST BIN ROTA

	January	April	July	October
Bin 1	Full – take out well-rotted compost for use in the garden and transfer remaining to bin 2	Empty	Empty	½ full
Bin 2	Empty	½ full	Full – take out well-rotted compost for use in the garden and transfer remaining to bin 1	Empty

IN THE SPRING

Spring sowing

There is a detailed, specific sowing and growing section for all the plants later in the book, but generally the processes are the same. Sowing and planting can begin indoors from December onwards. Boxing Day is traditionally the time when we sow onion seeds in readiness for planting the onions outdoors.

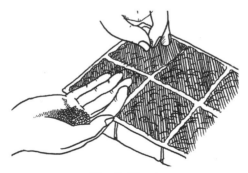

Fig. 7. Planting

Order seeds early

Cold winter nights can be profitably spent planning what you are going to grow. If you can buy seeds direct from the seed merchant, rather than waiting for the garden centre to rebuild their stock, you can ensure your crops will be planted on time. You will also have the best quality seeds; although supermarkets do stock seed in the early spring, I have found that often they have been under lights or in other unsuitable positions. Seed merchants always send out catalogues in gardening magazines and if you buy one in December or January you will have more catalogues than you need.

Storing seeds

Growing in pots and planters means that you do not need a lot of seed at any one time. You can store seeds, wrapped in their packets inside a lidded box or tin. I use an old tea tin with several pieces of kitchen paper to absorb any moisture. They must be stored in a cool, dry place, away from the possibility of vermin eating your stores. Warm seed does not last long as bacterial and fungal infections can take hold more easily. Seeds that have been stored well for a year will still germinate at 95% the rate of brand new ones, though two years old is somewhat hit and miss. Of course their growing properties depend on the how well they have been stored.

What kind of seeds should I get?

F1 Hybrid seeds

A small genetics lesson: if you pollinate one plant with another, the offspring might have some of the characteristics of both. But if you cross all the offspring, around 25% will resemble one grandparent, 25% will resemble the other grandparent and 50% will resemble their parents. In other words, you will notice that not all the plants will reproduce truly. F1 hybrids are the first hybrid grown from two separate plants. F2 is the the product of the first hybrid, and F3 the second and so on. F1 are usually very successful plants as long as you do not wish to collect the seeds from your plants to save for next year, since a quarter of your yield will not resemble the rest. F1 hybrids usually have vigour not normally found in the other types; they grow quickly and often have a more developed disease resistance.

PELLETED SEED

Seeds that are surrounded with a water-absorbent coating material provide the grower with a number of options. Firstly, the seed is bigger and easier to handle. The pellet that surrounds the seed is impregnated with anti-fungal agents and a little fertiliser. Secondly, they have an increased and rapid germination to seedlings because of their fertiliser content and a more consistent germination because of the fungicide. The downside is the increased cost.

Annuals, biennials and perennials

When working in pots and containers we more or less treat everything as annuals. What I mean by this is we sow seeds in spring and consume the plant in a single year, even if the plant would normally live for more than one year. Onion seeds will grow into an onion in year 1 and then go to seed in year 2. Onion sets, those tiny onions you can buy and push into the ground, have grown for one year and then are frozen to kill the flower bud. When you grow them they simply become large onions and never flower.

Plants like asparagus (YES! It is possible to grow asparagus on a patio) are planted as a crown into compost that is refreshed each autumn. Rhubarb similarly.

Indoor seed sowing

In the late winter and early spring the garden comes indoors while we start seeds off either in trays or modules or the paper pots we described earlier. The most common way of starting seeds is in propagators, which take many forms.

PROPAGATORS

A simple plastic tray, around 36cm by 22cm, with a close-fitting plastic lid to maintain the air temperature and humidity around the seedling and more importantly to cut out draughts of cold air, can be bought for very little money. They are quite flimsy and do not withstand a lot of handling. Years ago they used to be made from wood, and if you have any of these you are lucky indeed. They are so elegant compared with modern plastic structures.

If you are buying new trays, try to go for the more rigid ones because they will last longer, and at around 40p each they are good value compared with flimsy ones that last only a season and are almost as expensive.

HEATED PROPAGATORS

Electronically controlled propagators with under-soil heating are expensive to buy but do create exact results. They are usually fitted with a lid and hold up to three standard-sized trays. You can set the temperature to exactly what it says on the seed packet for germination.

Usually, though, heated propagators cater for only standard-sized trays and consequently they are no use for plant pots and other non standard-sized containers.

HEATED MATS

You can buy a rubberised mat, which is a little like an electric blanket but is used to stand a propagator tray on. These are less exact than the heated propagator, but far cheaper. Again you can set the temperature exactly and since they are double insulated you don't have to worry about minor water spillage.

HEATING CABLE

You can also buy insulated heating cable. This is slightly less easy to control, but still enables you to alter the temperature. You need a large tray with a deep lip for this method. In the tray place about an inch or two of sand, on top of which the heating cable is coiled. Then you cover it with another inch or two of sand. You place your propagator trays on top of this. The seeds receive a gentle heat from the sand.

Some seed trays come with grooves that are supposed to be designed for fitting heating cable into them. I tend to ignore this design completely, preferring to bury the cable in sand as described, mainly for ease of use but also because the sand spreads the heat much more evenly and gently.

COLD FRAMES

Every patio can afford space for a cold frame. If you are sowing cabbages or other plants that do not need much in the way of heat, buy or build a small cold frame. The lid will make it draught-free and the greenhouse effect will keep the plants warm during the day. You can heat these easily at night by simply fitting a night light candle into the space of a hollow concrete block. This is more than enough to keep the frost away.

What to avoid

Try to set your seeds off in as even a temperature as you can. However tempted you are, keep the trays of seedlings away from radiators and other domestic heaters. One lady I knew put a glass box (a large homemade affair) around the flue of her domestic boiler to grow plants in, thinking she would benefit from all that lost heat. She was lucky that her contraption was noticed before she filled her house with poisonous gases.

Do not keep the seedlings too hot. If you have to cool them down by watering, they are too hot. Too much heat brings with it two other problems. Excessive growth in the first days of growth can lead to weaker stems which can pose problems when it comes to the transplanting stage. Secondly, too much heat leads to water evaporation and consequently water stress. Young cells can burst very easily in seedlings and this can lead to infection problems in the first month of life.

HUMIDITY

If the seedlings are in a draught-free place, when they have definite leaves in place, lift the lid for some time during the day to allow excess moisture-laden air to escape. This way the seedlings will grow stronger and you will be able to avoid the fungal infections so often encouraged by excess moisture.

THE AIRING CUPBOARD

Many people have discovered the airing cupboard is a good place to start seedlings off. This is fine for the actual germination process, but as soon as leaves peep from the compost surface, bring the plants into the light. Many people remember that seedlings grow quickly in the dark, a phenomenon known as etiolation. But this growth is at the expense of the seedling and not only do they grow taller, they become progressively weaker too.

Preparing the compost for seed sowing

I have found over the years that the more care you take with seedlings, the better they will be once they are grown. What follows refers to propagator trays and we will come back to the other pots, modules and trays later.

MAKING SEED COMPOST

Seed compost has some benefits over multi-purpose compost. It is finer, it drains more easily and is eventually easier to transplant from. If you are going to make seed compost from homemade supplies you ought to sterilise the basic material first. An old baking tray is ideal for this. Fill the tray with compost and then put it in the oven at 125°C (Gas ½) for 20 minutes.

My recipe for seed compost is 75% sieved compost (you can use a colander if you don't have a riddle) 15% garden sand and 10% vermiculite. You can buy vermiculite from the garden centre.

FILLING THE TRAY

Fill the tray with seed compost to a depth of around an inch (2.5cm). Press this down firmly with a small piece of ply wood. I have a piece of wood that fills the tray exactly. You need to get a firm base so that if you were to touch it with your fingers you would not disturb the material.

On top of this fill with more compost to about half an inch (1cm) from the top of the tray. This is firmed again, but not so strongly as before. You are looking for a neat finish that you can mark or punch holes in or simply lay seeds on top.

MARKING OUT

When using trays I like to mark the compost as a guide to sowing. Simply mark out a grid with a fine point such as a pencil or dibber, so you have squares that are around 2cm over the surface. The times when you simply broadcast seeds over the surface of the compost are few indeed. Usually only cress is sown in this way. For everything else you will benefit from some structure in the way you sow.

WETTING

Once the compost is firmed in and marked out it is time to introduce water, the one substance needed to make the seeds burst into life. This is done by floating the tray in a bowl of water (the washing up bowl is useful here) until it can be seen seeping through to the surface and everything is visibly wet. Lay the tray on one side and allow it to drain any excess.

SOWING LARGE SEEDS

If you are starting off peas and beans indoors (and we will look at other ways of sowing these plants in later chapters), soak the seeds in water overnight. Use water at a temperature of around 10C, any colder will stop the growth of the plants. This goes for whenever you water the seedlings too – a douse of cold water will only cause the plants to stop growing. Preferably use rainwater than tap water because some of the chemicals added to tap water can kill off some of the beneficial microbes on the seeds.

A large seed should be pushed under the surface every 2 inches/5cm. Create a small hole about ¾ inch/2cm deep with a pencil and place a seed in each. Sprinkle the tray with sieved compost and firm down to maximise the seed's contact with the damp compost.

Place the lid on the propagator and leave it alone. The seeds will not need watering for some time. Within a week you should start to see the first leaves pushing through the compost. At this point give them a small sprinkle of water. If you can buy or clean out a plastic bottle that delivers a fine spray, all the better. Alternatively, water with a fine rose or give a soaking from underneath. The rose is the sprinkler at the end of the watering can (you can get watering cans with different sized holes) – it needs to be rose really or else gardeners will laugh.

When the plants have started germination you might find there are one or two places where the seed hasn't germinated. You can carefully move the compost to see if the seed is showing signs of germination and if necessary remove the old seed and pop in another.

For many plants it is customary to plant two seeds together and reject the slowest growing, but we will come back to that when we talk about sowing in pots.

SOWING SMALL SEEDS

If you are growing in pots and containers, it isn't always possible to mimic the big garden world. For example, many small seeds are sown in drills. A drill is a scrape in the soil around about 3 inches/8cm deep in a straight line – we often call a line of soldiers a drill, and we talk about doing drill, by which we mean working in straight lines.

Fig. 8. Drainpipe carrot

Carrots in sawn off drainpipes Many plants that bear small seeds, such as carrots, do not take to being transplanted (you end up with all kinds of strange shapes) so the thing to do is to sow them where they will grow. And of course this depends on what you are growing and what you are growing in. What follows assumes you are growing carrot seeds in sawn off drainpipes.

The drainpipe will be as deep as you want the carrot to grow, and split in half length ways so you have two halves that are tied or taped together. Block off the bottom of the pipe with tape, or you can simply stand the tube on the floor or in an old pot. Remember to pierce the base so that it can drain. You need to load it with compost in the same way as for any seed. Give it a good soaking with water from above with a fine rose watering can.

Personally, I worry about whether a single tiny seed will germinate and I sow a small number – around three and then sprinkle some compost on the top, firming down. You can make a fine local climate for the seeds by placing a clear plastic bag over each tube and hold it in position with an elastic band.

Sowing radishes in trays Growing radishes can be a little tricky because they need to be transplanted early so you do not get misshapen plants, but they grow in all kinds of situations from hanging baskets to single pots. They serve here to illustrate broadcast sowing in a tray.

Prepare your tray of compost and mark it out as mentioned previously. You are aiming to get around 30 marked out sections on the compost. I try not to handle seeds too often so I use the packet to carefully sprinkle around three seeds per section on the surface of the compost. Then finish off by sprinkling compost on top and firming down. You should have a series of seedlings clumped together in each section but also spread evenly over the tray.

Sowing cabbages in modules You can buy seed trays already divided into compartments known as modules. The idea is that you fill each module with compost and then push your finger through the bottom of the flimsy plastic to get the plant out.

Treat the modules exactly the same way as a seed tray and sow three cabbage seeds into each one. Then allow them to germinate and when the plants are healthily large select only a single plant in each module. This is the healthiest looking, not necessilary the largest. This selection is made by simply pulling the other two plants out and allowing the final one to grow.

Sowing cabbages in drinking cups I save drinks cups or yoghurt pots, and even buy them especially for the job. I use the thick insulated polystyrene cups and I pierce through the bottom for drainage, without making a large hole – a crack is enough. I then make a layered compost in the usual way, using another cup to pat the compost down. The bottom of the pot is filled with 50:50 mixture of compost and lime. I fill about the bottom third of the cup with this mixture, then top up with good, rich compost. Firm down and wet in the usual way.

Sow three seeds in each and select the best growing plant. The beauty of these pots is that the seeds will grow for ages, right into the summer if you want them before you place your cabbages into their final growing positions.

How to transplant – pricking out

There are many different types of seedling and you will have to depend on the seed packet for very specific instructions. Many plants need to be taken from the seed tray to a second pot and from there to a third pot and so on. Pricking out is an important skill akin to minor surgery in the potting shed, or the kitchen window if that's all you have.

TWO KINDS OF LEAVES

Most plants that need pricking out are known as dicotyledons, which means they appear from the seed with two first seed leaves. The other group – monocotyledons appear with only one. The first pair of seed leaves produced by dicotyledons are usually a completely different shape from the true leaves they produce next.

These first leaves eventually shrivel away, but just as the second leaves are appearing they can be used as a convenient handle to prick out the plants.

GET ORGANISED

Organisation is key for successful transplantation. If you have everything ready, your job will be all the easier. In the transplantation of radishes (a good example of dicotyledons), you need to have your pot ready to receive the seedlings with firmed compost in place, already wet. With a pencil (a pencil is by far the best tool for the job) make small 1cm/½ inch round holes about 3cm/1½ inches deep in your pot. The holes in this case should be spaced at around 6cm/2½ inches for the plants to grow.

In the seed tray, choose the seedlings you are going to prick out. They should be robust plants, without blemish or deformity. Carefully push your pencil through the compost next to the plant and holding only the leaf as a guide, not as a handle, lever the seedling out of the compost. USE THE PENCIL to do the moving and pull only lightly on the leaf. NEVER, HANDLE THE STEM. Even the lightest pressure on the stem will kill the plant.

Carry the seedling to the prepared hole in the pot and use the pencil to guide the rootlet carefully into the hole. Then gently infill the hole with compost using the fingers and pencil. Lightly firm the seedling in place and water with a fine mist spray. Cover the new pot with a clear plastic freezer bag and place it in a cool but draught-free place. Within a few days the seedlings should be growing normally.

Incidentally, with this spacing in a large pot the plants will grow rapidly and soon begin to crowd each other. I remove every other radish plant when the pot looks full and use them in salads and stir fry meals, allowing space for the rest to grow – but more of that later!

POTTING ON

As already mentioned, it is sometimes possible to plant seeds in paper pots and simply place this pot into its final growing position. However, sometimes it is necessary to pot on from one sized pot to the next. This is frequently done with tomatoes. You will have sown in a tray, pricked out the seedlings into an 8cm/3 inch pot and from there into a 12cm/6 inch pot before finally placing the plant into its final growing position.

This is done to keep the plants secure in the pot, to encourage a strong root ball and not allow the plant to grow too leggy, or long in the stem. Potting on is easier if you have grown them in plastic pots to begin with. You need to prepare your second pot to receive the plant. Simply fill to a depth of ⅓ of the pot with good compost. You might want to use a soil-based compost at this stage, incorporating maybe a little of the fungal hyphae (the thread-like filaments making up the fungus) some plants need, as we have already discussed.

Pots go up in steps With some exceptions, like the radish we planted out earlier, you should plant only into the next size pot, and not simply use a huge container. You allow only a little extra space for the plant to grow into because this keeps the roots in a good ball, rather than spreading out and becoming leggy as this opens them up to the possibility of damage and decay.

How to know when to pot on This is something of a judgement you need to get used to making. If the plant is about ⅔ of the size of the pot then it is around the right time to pot on. Look under the pot; if you see a little root peeping through the drainage hole, it is time to pot on.

TRANSFERRING THE PLANT

Simply rub your plastic pot through your hands to loosen the compost round the edges a little. Cup the open end, hold the plant very gently between the fingers and turn the plant upside down. Tap firmly on the base of the pot and pull it off. The plant should come loose.

Without teasing the roots (something you see gardeners doing on the television and is quite wrong as tearing the roots is detrimental to the plant), place the plant into its new pot centrally and fill in the gap between the compost and the wall of the new pot. Carefully, but firmly, press the new plant into position and water with 10°C water from a can with a fine-holed rose.

Spring jobs

The following should be used as a quick guide to help you remember the many spring tasks, between March and the end of April.

Job	Variety	Cropping
Sow under cover	Broccoli	Up to 125 days
	Summer cauliflower	July onwards
	Summer cabbage	August onwards
	French bean	June onwards
	Runner bean	July
	Sweetcorn	September
	Tomatoes	August onwards
Sow outdoors	Beetroot	June onwards
	Brussels sprouts	September onwards
	Carrots	June onwards
	Main crop onions	August
	Spring onion	June onwards
	Main crop peas	July
	Lettuce	June onwards
	Shallots	August

Plant outdoors	Main crop potatoes	July–August onwards
	Onion sets	August onwards
	Strawberries	June onwards
Harvest	Parsnip	
	Wintered spring onion	
	Beets and kale	
	Spring ripening lettuce	
	Cauliflower	
Feed	All container-grown fruit	
Pests and diseases	Young slugs and snails	
	Birds	
	Pea moths	
	Aphids	
Protect	Fruit blossom from frost, birds and cold winds by draping plants with fleece	
	All fruit against fungal infection by spraying with Bordeaux mixture	

Maintenance	Item	Special requirements
Ventilate	Open cold frames	On warm days open up your cold frames to give air to the hardening-off seedlings. Close them at night.
Prepare	Make homemade manure by filling a pillowcase of well-rotted manure, tying off and soaking in a water butt.	

IN THE SUMMER

The delicate change from spring to summer brings with it many special jobs for the patio grower, that are quite different from those facing the deep soil gardener. Fruit trees in particular need special attention at this time, as the roots are restricted because of the pot. This causes the plant to become restricted itself, and in the case of apple trees particularly, you need to feed the plant in early summer to avoid lots of June drop. This is where the plant discards a quantity of the young developing fruit as it grows only what it needs, and so the fruit falls. During May, feed all the fruit with a multi-purpose fertiliser and, if you can, de-compact some of the compost in the container and add a mulch to protect the surface of the soil.

Leaf trimming

If there is a drought coming along, you need to have a plan for watering. Check your pots every day for moisture content and be sure you never let plants dry out completely. If you are going away, or are at work all day you might consider if it is important to reduce the plants' ability to transpire. If the plant has a smaller area, it cannot transpire so much water. Large leafed plants such as lettuce and cabbage transpire a large amount. Reducing the leaf area by half will stop this. It works particularly well with lettuce. You can eat the cuttings and leave the plant better able to deal with drought.

Dealing with pests

On the patio there is a number of pests you have to look out for more vigilantly than in the garden, some easily dealt with, some are a little trickier.

SLUGS AND SNAILS

On the patio these molluscs are fewer in number than in the garden but they do come along to the patio in search of food. They are extremely acrobatic and will climb over other plants to get to the plants they want. They are fewer in number because they lay eggs in the soil and remain there in huge numbers, sometimes many hundreds of thousands in each garden. However, on the patio you are going to encounter only strays.

I firmly believe bait, the normal slug pellet, should not be left on the patio because it is more readily available for pets, birds and mammals to eat. The biological control methods for dealing with them do work, but not so effectively. There is a number of nematode worm preparations that, when diluted and sprinkled, infect slugs and kill them. However, with small pots they are easily washed away and a cold night will kill the nematodes, thus making them difficult to use.

The basic, successful way of dealing with slugs and snails depends on making a barrier from the mollusc to the plant. You can put a line of salt around the pots and planters.

This kills the snails and you have to clear them away. A second way is to put the pots on a surface they do not like. Sandpaper works well enough, but is expensive. You can buy a product made from sheep's wool that works quite well too, but the one with a 100% success rate on my patio is to stand the pots on copper rings. The animals get an unpleasant shock from the copper as their moist bodies make an electric cell.

APHIDS

Aphids, mostly greenfly and blackfly, cause all sorts of problems in the garden from wilting plants to creating fungal and viral infections. They use their mouthparts to pierce the tubes in the stem that carries sugar from the leaves to the rest of the plant. This syrup is under high pressure and gushes through the insect and pours all over the plant as a liquid known as honeydew.

Aphids survive on any number of vegetables from lettuce to cabbage – anything with flesh soft enough for their mouthparts to pierce, and once a lone insect lands on its host, it reproduces to produce an infestation within hours.

Aphids survive the winter as eggs and appear as small adults in the spring. The first adult is wingless and she gives birth without mating to dozens of smaller versions of herself. When the numbers build up, some of these offspring produce wings and fly off to another host, often mating on the way to lay eggs. Some aphids produce alternate generations of wingless and winged forms. By these methods they very quickly take advantage of the new vegetable growth in the garden.

Aphid problems The boring mouthparts of the insect cause damage inside the plant and in the process they break many water-bearing tubes in the stem. If enough are pierced, the plant begins to fall over or wilt.

Honeydew promotes fungal infections as spores fall on the plant from the air and grow rapidly in the sugary syrup. Some botrytis and filamentous grey moulds are attributable to aphids. Grey mould becomes a particular problem on tomatoes and cucumbers grown in greenhouses and polytunnels. Also, plant viruses are spread around the garden by aphids. Economically this is important and can knock out many of your lovingly-grown crops, particularly fruit.

Treatments for aphids Of course you could spray your plants with all sorts of poisons to kill aphids on the patio. You can buy hand-pumped sprays diluted to the right strength and all you have to do is treat your plants. This is possibly the most effective control method but perhaps not the best for garden and personal health. No matter how safe the manufacturers say they are, I personally cannot bring myself to spray my food with complex chemicals, so I prefer a more organic method.

The easiest way to remove aphids is to rub them off with your thumb and finger, but it is perhaps a little messy. Spraying them with a high-powered jet with a hint of simple soap in the water dissolves the waxy covering on the insect and they simply dry out and die.

You can also buy lacewings and ladybirds, especially online. The adults and grubs of both these insects eat lots of greenfly, but I have never seen them actually keep plants free from infestation.

BLIGHT

Blight is a devastating disease of the Solanaceae, which means that both potatoes and tomatoes get it, as well as some plants in the flower garden.

It is caused by a fungus and comes in two forms; early, which hardly causes any problems at all, and late. Late blight is a serious headache because you can lose your spuds and tomatoes too, all in the course of a single day!

It takes hold of your crop within 24 hours and comes once the rain has interrupted a week or so of glorious weather. The first signs are big black splodges on the leaves and then the blackening of the whole plant. This can happen in just a few hours and you have to work fast to save your crop.

Just check On the leading edge of the black spots you can see little white hairs. If you see these, you have blight. These are the fruiting bodies of the fungus.

Even if there are just a few spores on a wet potato, they are doomed.

Conditions for growth In July, when you get warm weather, any rain will create just the right humid conditions necessary for blight to grow. Be careful just to water at soil level, not damping the leaves at all. Recent research has shown that the fungal spores occur at the highest concentration in the splash zone where water and mud accumulate on the stalks of the plants. In the greenhouse, water tomatoes very carefully, preferably in a pot beside the plant.

In the second or third week of July, cut out some of the potato vines, just to improve ventilation around the plants.

Control Firstly, do not save potatoes for growing next year. Plant new stock, preferably varieties with high disease resistance. Plant them thinly, and make sure there's a lot of ventilation space around each vine, so that the microclimate for each plant doesn't remain hot and moist.

Secondly, avoid watering the plants over the leaves, water only at compost level, this will help control humidity, and stop spores washing from the leaves to the soil.

You need to cut off the vines at soil level without disturbing the roots. BURN the vines, don't compost them. Then give the soil a treatment of disinfectant, go and change your clothes, have a good wash and then pull up the tubers. Wipe them dry and store them on a shelf in a dry, cool place. Then hope for the best. If they have remained uninfected a week later they should be still sound. Otherwise they will be black and mushy. Make sure there is plenty of air around each potato.

Always disinfect your hands and tools before going from the potato patch to the greenhouse to prune the tomatoes and visa versa. Remember, it's more humid in the greenhouse and therefore blight is more easily spread.

Research has shown that copper-based fungicides have no impact on this disease, so washing with things such as Bordeaux mixture is of little value.

DAMPING OFF

This is a strange-sounding name for a plant pest but it is actually a very common fungal disease. It is to be found in soil and attacks the stems of young plants and seedlings. This occurs mostly in humid conditions and high temperatures. It is much more prevalent in the spring, when new seedlings emerge, but is also found when you plant on patios because the tendency to water more increases the humidity and consequently increases the chances of the disease. The fungal spores are found on all kinds of surfaces.

What damping off looks like Seedlings and young plants suddenly collapse at the surface of the compost. There are lots of fungal hairs (or hyphae) all over the plant and it is these that distribute the spores. Once the plants are infected there is nothing you can do to get them to recover.

Control Make sure your trays and pots are sterilised with a garden disinfectant. Try to sow thinly so as to reduce the humidity around each plant. You can water with a quarter-strength solution of a copper-based fungicide, Bordeaux mixture. This has been used for many hundreds of years and, until recently, has been a recognised organic treatment.

VINE WEEVILS

Hardly known fifty years ago, the vine weevil has come into prominence because of the number of container-bought plants that have, over the years, been sold from garden centres. Weevil attack is increasing not only in tubs and patio plants but in polytunnels, and in beds and plots. As more plants are grown abroad and shipped into the UK this problem is going to increase over the next few years, particularly as new species of weevil arrive that have no real predators.

The adult weevil feeds on leaves of almost every plant going, but hardly eats enough to cause anything more than an unsightly semicircular notch. The larvae feed voraciously on roots and can damage plants enough for them to die. They particularly like young roots with the consequence that spring-growing plants are particularly susceptible.

Most species of vine weevil are almost entirely female. All the eggs laid by these individuals are genetically identical to their mother. Weevils are flightless but very good at walking and consequently spread around the garden easily. They can climb the vertical faces of flowerpots — even the plastic ones.

If you notice a leaf with a little semicircular notch on it you can guarantee there are weevil eggs in the soil near the roots. The symptoms of larval attack are yellowing leaves and wilting plants that do not respond to watering. You are almost sure to have lost the plant, but you might try shaking the compost off the roots and replanting.

The grubs are frequently dug out of the soil and look like a greyish white caterpillar that invariably holds itself bent double. I must confess that if I kill anything in the garden, I make sure it is not wasted. Simply put the grub on the path and by the time you have gone inside a bird will have eaten it.

Control of vine weevils Vine weevils are controlled in a number of ways. You can try growing sacrificial plants that the grubs prefer to eat, such as primula, polyanthus and cyclamen. These plants, when grown around your crops, will attract the adults away from your growing area.

There is a number of products that use nematodes to kill grubs in the soil. *Steinernema kraussei* works down to 8°C while *Heterorhabditis megidis* works a little warmer. Products such as Nemasys are widely available and work well if you make sure you follow the instructions.

Finally, because the adults are nocturnal, leave traps of cardboard egg boxes for them to rest under during the day. It is surprising how many you can catch.

A WORD ABOUT BIOLOGICAL CONTROL

Organic growing is best on the patio It might be that you are used to what is called conventional gardening, that is to say using poisons against insects and other pests in the garden. However, there are some good reasons for using organic principles wherever you can on the patio.

The problem with growing in pots and containers is that you need to water more frequently, feed more often and use more fertiliser, and consequently, you would probably use more chemicals – and in the end plants would accumulate more. No matter how safe people say certain chemicals are, I have always worried about the safety of such chemicals for growing vegetables on the patio. I am sure there will be some people who will applaud this comment and possibly just as many who will say I am some sort of green freak. So be it, I just worry that's all.

But that doesn't mean that we just have to lie down and allow Mother Nature to bring all her creation to our patio for a good dinner every day. There are alternatives to using chemicals on the patio.

Biological control Whatever you say about it, biological control doesn't work as effectively as a chemical in the garden. But it is possible to make it work more effectively on the patio – except for slugs and snails. But then there are other ways of doing this as we have already said.

The problem in the garden is that it is too big and difficult to control. A box full of ladybird larvae in a garden is not going to gobble all the aphids there, and by the time they have lumbered up the infected plant a second generation of winged insects has already legged it to the next part of the garden. But on the patio you can box clever. You can put a plastic bag around plants you are treating and then allow the biological control plants to get on with their job.

On the patio, which is much more compact than the ordinary garden, there is more chance of concentrating biological control methods than in the garden. Consequently there is a better chance of making it work at a reasonable cost.

Pest	Product	Notes
Aphids	Aphidoletes	Best in the greenhouse
	Aphidius	As above
Mealy bug	Cryptolaemus	Ladybird
	Hypoaspis	
	Leptomastix	Best in greenhouse
Red spider mite	Phytoseilius	
	Phytoline	
	Control 2000	

Sciarid fly	Hypoaspis	
Scale insects	Scale nematodes Metaphycus	Needs to be kept moist
Slugs	Nemaslug Slugsure	Use from March, when the soil is over 5°C As above
Slugs and snails	Organic Bio Stimulant	This deters slugs, they don't like the smell
Vine Weevil	Nemasys	Use from March, when the soil is over 5°C

Summertime jobs

Job	Variety	Cropping
Sow outdoors	Lettuce	July onwards
	Peas	August
	Carrots	August/September
	Beetroot	August
	Marrow	September
	Courgettes	Late summer
	Spinach	Late summer
	Salad onions	Autumn
	Chinese Brassicas	Spring, or as soon as they look edible
	Carrots – Autumn King	Autumn
	Carrots – Chantenay	Winter
	Chicory	Winter onwards
	Lettuce	All the time
	Winter onions	Spring
	Salad onion	Autumn onwards
	Turnip	Autumn
	Spring cabbage	Winter

Plant outdoors	Potatoes – late in May	Autumn
	Potatoes – August and bring indoors for Christmas	Christmas
Plant indoors	Tomatoes	Summer
Crop	Asparagus	Use a knife just under the soil
	All salad crops	
	Strawberries	
	Rhubarb	
	First cabbages	
	Early potatoes	

IN THE AUTUMN

The patio gardener has a lot to do in autumn, especially harvesting and preparing plants for the winter, helping them to grow for longer on the patio so that you don't *have* to harvest them, and of course, planning for next year too.

It is time to plant garlic

The autumn is time to plant garlic, and the more ways you can find to grow it, the better. I like to grow garlic in rich compost in the holes of breeze blocks, in pots all over the garden, around the edge of planters to act as guardsmen protecting the planting inside.

I plant a lot of garlic simply to disguise the other plants. Since I like garlic I don't mind the odd taint some crops pick up. The garlic for this purpose, I simply use from the supermarket, breaking up corms from the ones we might eat. However, plants destined for the kitchen I buy specially. Although supermarket corms do grow well, they never attain the size or the quality of those plants grown specially for the UK climate.

Jerusalem artichokes, rhubarb and horseradish can all be planted in the autumn, preferably before November. Artichokes and horseradish can both be invasive when grown in bare soil, but a large pot is excellent – particularly for the horseradish.

Artichokes need a much larger tub. All enjoy well-drained, rich soil, so work as much manure or organic matter you can.

Growing in a wheelie bin

A bank of wheelie bins make perfect growing containers for a number of crops. They are made even more useful by cutting a chunk from the bottom of the front with a saw, but be careful! Try to cut a piece that is at least 18 inches/50cm high. This can be taped back into position to stop the compost falling out. Then you can think about planting crops in it. In this instance, and the reason for mentioning it in the autumn, is to plant artichokes in the bin.

The lid is left down after a couple of tubers are planted in the soil-based compost that fills about ¾ of the bin. In the spring, the lid of the bin is opened when the plant is seen pushing itself up through the compost. Keep it watered, with a little soluble feed, and the plant will grow very large out of the bin.

In October, open the door and pull out the tubers, keeping the compost, which can be enriched with well-rotted manure to grow potatoes in exactly the same way.

Get some manure

If you have the space, place a bulk-order for manure and leave it to rot down over the winter. If you have a choice, use horse manure for heavy soils, cow for lighter conditions.

Apples, pears and gooseberries

After the apple harvest, prune both apples and pears, but be careful not to prune them too heavily. I reduce the branches by only a third of their length. Trees grown in pots, on dwarfing rootstocks, will not grow too high or extensive anyway. You run the risk of making the plant unproductive by heavy pruning.

Prune gooseberries, if you don't have a problem with birds. If you do, then put this off until March otherwise they'll steal all the buds. Take any crowded side-shoots down to two or three buds, leaving any that are in the right place at full length. When pruning, remember the aim is to have an open centre in each bush, to make it easier to pick the fruit later in the year.

Pests

Place nets over brassicas to protect them from pigeons, indeed all your appetising crops such as salads, late carrots and onions. Remove dead leaves from brassicas to keep infections down and press in sprouts to keep the buttons firm on the plant. This is the most important job if you want an edible crop.

Move the plants that are still in production nearer to the house wall. Leeks grown in pots will do especially well because they become soft and mushy if they are too frosted when grown in pots.

Cleanliness in the garden

The human foot is responsible for moving more disease around the patio than any other means. Get yourself a few planks and walk on only these while you give your patio stones a good cleaning.

Pick up your rubbish and burn it. It is remarkable how much rubbish falls behind pots and containers that we have become used to looking at. If it has spent some time lying on the ground then it isn't worth composting. Have a bonfire and use the ashes in compost, mixed with leaf mulch, or keep aside for later use (it actually makes great cat litter).

Wildlife

Make sure you check for hedgehogs when working around the patio. Frogs and toads are also vulnerable, and if you keep a pond, make sure it is leaf- and rubbish-free. When it gets cold the first instinct for frogs is to head for water, where they sit out the winter in the mud at the bottom, but if there are lots of rotting leaves there, the oxygen content of the water will not be enough to support life.

Wash and disinfect bird feeders and, through the winter and spring, keep them filled regularly. Do not allow any fallen seeds or fat to remain because it will cause fungi to grow which will eventually kill more birds than having no food at all.

For me it is important that we do not sit in judgement on the wildlife that visits our gardens. Some people, for some inexplicable reason, prefer blue tits over magpies and I can't understand why, especially if we feed them well enough. Yes, magpies eat baby blue tits, but why should this be reason enough for us to discourage them with stones? Similarly, squirrels are persecuted to the expense of song birds; well, not in my garden.

CHAPTER 5

HOW TO GROW VEGETABLES ON THE PATIO

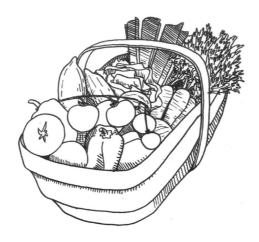

The following is a comprehensive A-Z guide to growing the most popular vegetables on the patio.

GROWING ASPARAGUS

Normally this plant needs a lot of space and the way it grows is to build an underground stem which then throws out little stalks in the early summer, which we eat. Then some of the stems, also known as spears, are allowed to grow for the year so that the plant grows stronger. It dies back in the winter.

They should be planted in March and a container with an area of around 1m by 1m is important. Prepare the pot by filling ⅓ with compost, then create a small mound in the centre. The plants come as 'crowns', which is a rhizome or underground stem. Tease out the roots to make an upturned 'V' shape and then spread over the mound. The whole plant is then buried in rich loamy compost. You need to plant crowns at a distance of around 1m or 3ft apart in the ground, so only one plant per pot.

You will need a large, deep container for growing asparagus on a patio, as you need plenty of space to allow the plant to throw up a lot of spears. They grow quite a large plant, so you must allow for this. I have grown it in a purpose-built brick chamber, 2m by 1m/6ft by 3ft at a depth of around 2ft/60cm. You can also grow this plant in the soil underneath the patio by raising a paving stone or two.

Container-grown asparagus can work if you have a large space to work with. I have used an old chest freezer and an old corrugated washtub before now. The important thing is to try to replace as much compost in the spring as you can without disturbing the plant. It can become a bit of an archaeological dig.

Once you have planted your crowns, allow the spears to grow so that the plant is very large. You might wish to provide support with a cane or two. Container-grown plants need to be fed fortnightly with a basic fertiliser. It will start to die back by October and you can remove the growth at soil level. Add a mulch of compost at this point, just to keep it warm until the summer. Allow the plant to grow normally for three years before taking the spears the following May. Stop taking spears in the third week of May and always make sure you allow the plant to grow out each year.

Container-grown asparagus does not particularly produce a large crop. This is a novelty patio plant with a divine flavour!

Asparagus at a glance

Pot size	Sow/Plant	Care	Harvest
Large – at least 1m²	March – outdoors	Feed fortnightly with basic fertiliser. Remove growth at soil level in October.	Allow to grow for three years, before harvesting in May

GROWING ARTICHOKES

Globe

This is a fun plant to grow on the patio; it's huge and prefers some support. In the past, I have grown them in a wheelie bin and the plant acted as a sail, with the wind dragging the whole lot down the patio. The secret is to grow them small. You do need a big container, but once the globes have appeared, cut them off and use them as a vegetable boiled whole, instead of growing them for their individual 'leaves'.

Buy them as plants from the nurseryman and plant them in loamy compost in April. They are heavy feeders and will need liquid feed fortnightly from May to August. Keep on top of the watering – they don't want to be too damp, but their large leaves draw a lot of water from the container. They can be harvested from July to August and they will die back in autumn, and the leaves can be composted. You then feed it up by replacing compost at the top of the container with new rich compost. After about four years you need to replace the plants with new ones.

Jerusalem

These are not like Globe artichokes at all; in fact, they grow in the ground like potatoes and you can almost treat them as such. In April, plant the tubers in large containers of compost. I use 50:50 compost and soil. Plant a single tuber in a 40cm/18inch deep pot. The shoots will push through the soil and the plant will grow up to 2m. You will need to provide support – I tend to grow them against a wall or heavy-duty trellis.

The plant needs to be fed through the growing period from May to August with a fortnightly feed. You can also introduce slow release fertiliser blocks to the soil. Since the plant is large, with a large leaf area, it tends to dry out easily and so you need to be vigilant with water.

In September, the leaves change colour, and the whole shoot can be removed and composted. The tubers will be fine in the pot until you need them.

Artichoke at a glance

Variety	Pot size	Sow/Plant	Care	Harvest
Globe	Large	April – outdoors	Feed regularly and check water levels daily	July–August
Jerusalem	Large	April – outdoors	Feed fortnightly and check water levels daily	September

GROWING AUBERGINES

These plants can be treated more or less like tomatoes. They are best sown indoors in April at around 18°C in trays and pricked out into individual 8cm/3 inch pots when large enough to handle. Pot them on into 12cm/6 inch pots and then transfer to their growing position. They need to be grown in a greenhouse or under a plastic cover/indoors. By the end of May they can be in their mini-greenhouses etc., but make sure the night-time temperature is going to be above freezing.

As I like to move them around, I tend to grow them one plant to a grow bag and stand this on its end, pushing the compost down to make a manageable shape. In July, pinch out the growing point, or the tip of the plant. This will force the plants to send out side shoots, which will bear flowers and consequently fruit.

Keep well watered and feed weekly with tomato fertiliser. Harvest the fruits when they are shiny by cutting them off the plant with a sharp knife.

Aubergine at a glance

Pot size	Sow/Plant	Care	Harvest
Medium – grow bags upturned on the side will work	April – indoors	Feed weekly and water daily	When fruits are large and shiny

GROWING BROAD BEANS

I prefer to grow dwarf broad beans on the patio, purely for space. On the allotment they grow in double rows to give each other support, but on the patio I grow them singly in 12 inch/30cm pots. I once inherited some large industrial containers which were 12 inch/30cm cubes. They stood together very easily and it was possible to line the far side of the patio with them, growing broad beans. I had 20 of them, but they broke over the years. You could upturn a grow bag as we have mentioned earlier. You can also grow them in old buckets – about the right size for a single plant. If you clump them together, around three or four, and add a cane to each pot, you can fashion a small teepee by tying them at the top.

Start the seeds off as early as October if you have a cool greenhouse, or in the warm from March. I tend to make newspaper pots for them and sow two seeds per pot, discarding the weaker seedling. The strong ones are then transferred directly to their final growing positions in late April for late-sown ones, November for early-sown ones.

The idea of sowing in October comes from allotment growing and on the patio is a little problematic. You need to protect the young plants from the rigours of the frost as in containers the plants are damaged more easily than in the soil. But the big advantage of sowing in October is that the plants grow very quickly when the weather improves. They set crop earlier and avoid the major infestation of blackfly, to which this vegetable is prone.

Keep the plants moderately watered and feed once a fortnight. When the flowers come in June you are a couple of months from cropping which takes place as soon as the pods start to change colour. You can take the pods when very young if you are going to cook them like mangetout.

Broad beans at a glance

Pot size	Sow/Plant	Care	Harvest
Very small – paper or plastic	March	Feed fortnightly and water moderately	August

GROWING FRENCH AND RUNNER BEANS

These need lots of organic matter for successful growing. I use a 50:50 mixture of compost and well-rotted manure. They can be grown almost hydroponically in very large plastic milk bottles. You need the large 4 litre bottles, opening the top of them by cutting across the lidded part of the bottle and adding four or five drainage holes. Fill this with the compost mixture and then sow a seed in each, keeping them indoors in February. They are extremely prone to frost damage, so wrap in fleece or bubble wrap if it is particularly cold, though the bottle affords a good amount of protection.

As the seedlings grow out of the bottles they will need to be watered and fed almost daily; I use a general purpose liquid feed when they are just growing, changing to a tomato feed once the leaves appear.

In May, take the bottles outdoors and tie them to the base of a trellis or a teepee of canes. As fruit appears, keep them fed and watered. Take the fruit as soon as they thicken in July, perhaps a little earlier in comparison with the soil-grown types. The more you pick them, the better they will crop.

Alternatively you can grow the plants in buckets or large pots, in which case they need to be watered and fed less. In essence, once the flowers are on the plant you cannot really over water/feed them as long as the roots have good drainage.

French and runner beans at a glance

Pot size	Sow/Plant	Care	Harvest
Medium – plastic milk bottles or buckets	February – indoors	Take outside in May, keep watered and fed daily	July

GROWING BEETROOT

This is one of the best plants to grow in a small space. Not only are the roots good to eat, the leaves and stems can be used too. I tend to sow them in March, in pots and containers of all sorts and then place them into a cold frame. I also sow wherever there is space for them from April onwards. They are the easiest things to sow; I make a scrape in the compost and sprinkle a number – goodness knows how many – of seeds into the compost and then cover over. As the seedlings grow I thin them out by pulling up every other one. These can then be used in salads.

For a successional crop, repeat the sowing/thinning process every fortnight until mid-August.

You can continue thinning until there is a hand-width between each plant, and then they can be allowed to grow to maturity. Pick the beetroots when they are between 2 inches/5cm in diameter, roughly cricket ball size.

If they are in single pots or small containers feed them every couple of weeks and try not to let them dry out because they will then become woody.

Fig. 9. Beetroot

Beetroot at a glance

Pot size	Sow/Plant	Care	Harvest
Medium	Late March–April	Feed fortnightly and do not allow to dry out	From July, or when bulbs are 5cm in diameter

GROWING BROCCOLI

This is an easy plant to grow in soil, not so simple in pots and containers. Sow seeds indoors in December. You can sow in a seed tray and transplant to 3 inch/8cm pots and thence to their final growing positions in April or May. In March, you can transfer them to a cold frame for the daylight hours and bring indoors at night. This is a process called hardening off.

The plant becomes quite leggy and lacks a lot of leaf when grown in pots. The roots like to be well firmed in and undisturbed, so to encourage healthy plants transplant them to 12 inch (30cm) pots while avoiding disturbing the roots. In the bottom of the pot put a layer of 1 inch (3cm) grit followed by a 3 inch (8cm) layer of 50:50 lime and compost. After this, place 50:50 compost/good soil mixture to within 2 inches (5cm) from the top. Plant one per pot and firm down the compost well.

Don't let the plant get troubled by wind, a sheltered spot is essential. Water to make sure the compost is mildly damp only – not too wet. Feed fortnightly with some liquid feed and keep firming in. Harvest as the heads form. You might find the heads a bit looser – that's one of the prices you pay for growing like this, but if you keep on firming, things should be fine.

Broccoli is a winter bearing plant – it takes quite a while for them to grow, but interestingly they are frequently ready more quickly on the patio.

Broccoli at a glance

Pot size	Sow/Plant	Care	Harvest
Small, transplant carefully into 12 inches (30cm) when grown	December	Feed fortnightly and ensure roots are well firmed in. Water lightly.	As soon as heads form

GROWING CABBAGE (SUMMER)

Cabbages are the oddest of all plants to grow in a pot or container. If you want round-headed cabbages you are best growing them in soil in a bed in the garden or allotment. You might get cabbage heads if you grow them individually in large pots, but they are much more likely to produce flowers and seeds. That said, they are perfectly edible, just different.

Start sowing in March in a cool greenhouse/cold frame. The idea is to keep the frost off, but not to worry too much about warmth. I grow in drinks cups for a little extra insulation. They are sown in a cup full of compost with a teaspoon of lime mixed in. Sow three or four seeds to a cup and remove all but the best-growing plants. Water with a fine film water spray, never let the compost dry, but do not over-water.

Another good way of starting cabbage seedlings is to plant 12 seeds in a 2 litre ice cream tub, thinning down to six. The cabbages are then removed from the tub by slicing the soil into segments, as if you were slicing a cake.

Try to plant on the cabbages into 12 inch (30cm) or larger pots and feed them fortnightly as well as making sure they are watered, especially when the weather is warm. Stress of any sort, overcrowding, drought, lack of minerals, will trigger the plant to explode into seed bearing, a process known as bolting or running to seed.

You can gather leaves whenever you need them, but normally you should take them as they heart up.

GROWING CABBAGE (AUTUMN)

Treat these as summer cabbages but sow them in late April to transfer into large pots or containers in May or June. They take much longer to mature and will be ready from September/October.

If you sow every three weeks from March with summer cabbage right through to the end of May with winter cabbage, you should be able eventually to get cabbage available most weeks of the year. Cabbages sown in August will provide an edible crop from December onwards.

Cabbage at a glance

Pot size	Sow/Plant	Care	Harvest
Medium – one per pot	March–May	Feed fortnightly and water frequently. Avoid stress of any type.	When plants heart up

GROWING CALABRESE

Treat as broccoli, but sow them in paper pots which are then transferred to their final growing positions. You can soak the paper and tear it to allow the roots access to the new compost. They do not like root disturbance at all and so you need to keep them in wind-free areas, well firmed in.

You can sow again in September, so you should be able to get an all-year round crop.

GROWING CARROTS

The carrot is the mainstay of the patio vegetable garden because it grows quickly and easily. They can be sown outdoors every week from March to September and you will never want for another carrot. They will grow in any container that will house compost from drainpipes to grow bags. In particular, they make a great edging plant and will grow happily in a grow bag turned onto its longest edge.

Like beetroot, simply sow carrot seeds liberally and thin them out as they grow, eating the thinnings in salads or as a garnish. You should end up with carrots spaced at 4 inches (10cm) apart. Water them regularly, especially in warm conditions. Feed them once every three weeks with liquid feed.

The only real problem with carrots is the carrot fly which appears around late April to June. Its presence varies according to locality. It flies at an altitude of around 18 inches (45cm) and cannot get much higher, so carrots lifted off the ground are perfectly safe. Inter-sow carrots with other crops from spring onions to marigolds to disguise them from this pest.

Carrots sown in September will be still growing in November, but will need some protection from the cold. I bring mine into my cold plastic lean-to greenhouse on really bad nights. The action of putting them against the wall of the house is frequently enough to keep them warm.

Carrots at a glance

Pot size	Sow/Plant	Care	Harvest
Small and long	March–September	Water regularly, feed every three weeks	From late May

GROWING CAULIFLOWER

Treat these exactly as cabbages, sowing and growing in the same way. The brassica family are all alike and you might find the cauliflower heads being loose, a bit like broccoli. They are best set in large 18 inch (45cm) pots and once set in place (in a sheltered but sunny spot), left alone apart from watering and feeding.

The heads will form and are best taken as soon as they are a couple of inches across and white. Once they get creamy they are past their best.

Cauliflower at a glance

Pot size	Sow/Plant	Care	Harvest
Medium – one per pot	March–May	Feed fortnightly and water frequently. Avoid stress of any type.	When heads form up to 2 inches

GROWING CELERIAC

Celeriac is a simple enough plant that has a mild celery flavour but quite a different texture. It is easily grown and will produce a crop much more easily than its distant cousin, celery. The plant grows into something that looks like a raggedy swede, but it isn't as tough.

Sow from February to April in compost at around 15°C (60°F) and prick out the plants when they are large enough into 3 inch (8cm) pots. Be patient with germination and it should take about a month to get to this stage. They don't like lower temperatures when being sown so if there is a cold spell, try to wait for a few days before sowing. This also goes for transplanting young plants to their final growing positions.

In June, plant the seedlings into 12 inch (30cm) pots, singly. Try to do this on a warm day if you can, otherwise they have a tendency to run to seed, especially if they have been shocked.

They prefer constant conditions and a nutrient-rich soil. Keep the soil moist but not wet, otherwise, once again, they will go to seed. Use well-rotted rich compost and the extra nutrients will keep the plant going.

When using celeriac, you are eating what is basically a swollen stem, but it will put out branches and side shoots from time to time, which should be removed. They can be harvested from September to the following spring. Cover them with fleece or straw in the coldest months but otherwise they are quite hardy.

The stem needs to be exposed to the air, so remove the lower leaves. Some people call this curing the stem but it isn't the same as curing meat. The exposure to the weather hardens the skin which in turn protects the stem.

Celeriac at a glance

Pot size	Sow/Plant	Care	Harvest
Medium – one per pot	February–April	Use rich compost and keep moist. Ensure a constant temperature.	September to March

GROWING CELERY

Generally any plant that produces a strong flavour has a complex metabolism going on inside to create it. Consequently, you need a lot of nutrients to achieve that flavour. The traditional way to grow celery is to dig a trench at least 2ft (60cm) deep and line it for months before planting with kitchen waste, like a little compost heap. The trench is then filled with 33% well-rotted manure, 33% compost and 33% soil.

However, in containers and pots this is not possible. I make up a manure/compost/soil mixture as above and fill 12 inch/30cm pots. The seeds are sown indoors in March. I use drinks cups with three seeds to a cup, thinning to only the best grower. This is transplanted to the pots at the end of May. You can bring your young plants outdoors from late April, bringing them indoors at night until mid-May. Then, in the last week before transplanting, so long as the weather is reasonable, keep them out all night.

Celery can be blanched if you want really white stalks. Simply cut open a tube of plastic (I have used old washing up bottles, when they weren't transparent!) and slip around the stalks.

Keep the plants well watered, and feed fortnightly with general purpose liquid feed. Take stalks when they are around 8 inches/20cm long. They are the archetypal cut-and-come-again plant.

Celery at a glance

Pot size	Sow/Plant	Care	Harvest
Medium – one per pot	March – indoors	Feed fortnightly and water regularly	When stalks are 8 inches tall

GROWING CHICORY

We miss out when we do not include chicory in our diet. The small swollen shoots are brilliant boiled and then added to pasta dishes, and as a bonus, the plant is easy to grow. It doesn't need to be bitter and anyone who has tried French coffee containing chicory, only to find it too harsh should not be put off this lovely plant.

Fill a large container or an 18 inch (45cm) pot with a mixture of 10% grit and the rest an equal mixture of well-rotted manure and compost. Make a drill 1 inch (2cm) deep that goes at least 2 inches (5cm) from the outer rim of the pot and sow the seeds thinly in May. You can sow them again in different pots every fortnight until the end of June.

The seeds should be thinned (as with most things partly grown, you can eat the thinnings) to leave a plant every 6 inches (18cm). Keep them in a sunny spot, and keep them well watered. Take the plants when the shoots are filling and a couple of inches tall, though this is smaller than would be found in the garden or allotment, and blanch them, thus reducing the bitter flavour, by putting an upturned plant pot over them.

Chicory at a glance

Pot size	Sow/Plant	Care	Harvest
Large	May	Water frequently and blanch to reduce bitterness	November

GROWING CHILLIES

In a way, you should treat the growing of chillies as though they were tomatoes. Sow chilli seeds between mid-February and mid-March. Germination can take a long time, so be patient. You need good multi-purpose compost but keep them free from soil.

Using trays that have been thoroughly wetted overnight, sow very thinly, around 1 inch/2cm apart and cover with dry compost. Firm down in the normal way. The temperature should be maintained at above 21°C, so you are probably best using a propagator to start them off. Make sure there is plenty of light.

Pot on progressively into 3 inch (8cm), then 6 inch (16cm), then 12 inch (30cm) pots.

Transfer to a greenhouse in June or July and water every couple or three days, feeding with tomato fertiliser at least twice a week. Take when the chillies are ripe in August/September.

Chillies at a glance

Pot size	Sow/Plant	Care	Harvest
Sow in trays, then pot on as necessary	Mid-Feb–March	Maintain temperature at 21°C	August–September

GROWING COURGETTES

Courgettes are robust yet delicate and are heavy feeders that can easily catch a chill. They crop very heavily but are prone to fungal disease. However, growing them on the patio does combat some of this.

The courgette needs plenty of rich soil, full of nutrients and moisture. They can be grown in large pots filled with a 50:50 mixture of well-rotted manure and compost. In late spring, possibly early May, you can buy courgette plants or sow them from late

March, early April . Sow two seeds per 3 inch (8cm) pot of multi-purpose compost and prick out the worst growers.

From May onwards, you can plant them into the prepared pots, allowing the leaves to train over the side of the pot. Keep them near the house at first, and move them to a sunny spot in June. If the weather is bad in May, a cloche can be used (an upturned lemonade bottle placed over like a mini-greenhouse, which works very well). By June, they can be left to the air.

You can also sow seeds directly into the pots in May, again two per pot, thinning out the weaker one. Cover with a bottle cloche and then let them grow through to mid-June before leaving them to the elements. Plant them on into 8 in (20cm) pots and leave to flower.

Courgettes have two flowers, one male and one female. They are usually pollinated by insects, but they can be helped. The female flower has a small courgette behind it, the male none. Take the male flower and with it brush the insides of the female flower with pollen. This way you will soon have good setting fruit. You can eat the flowers afterwards; they are wonderful deep fried!

The plants will now start to grow vigorously, needing plenty of water every couple of days. You can help the soil moisture by mulching, but try not to wet the plant when you water. Their only two major pests are slugs and a fungal infection, so keep the humidity down, while at the same time, water, water, water!

Cut the fruit with a sharp knife when they are about 12cm (5 inches). Don't let them grow into monsters unless you like them stuffed, as the flavour is not improved.

Courgette at a glance

Pot size	Sow/Plant	Care	Harvest
Medium	May	Water every other day, avoiding humidity	When 5 inches long

GROWING CUCUMBERS

Outdoor varieties are the best ones to grow on the patio because they are fairly easy and more robust, coping with all kinds of weather fluctuations. They are best grown against a trellis for support, and you can tie the fruits loosely to the structure, and nothing looks nicer too!

Sow 2 or 3 seeds per pot about an inch (2cm) deep. Discard all but the best growers and make sure you do not over water the plants. You can keep them indoors on a windowsill but they do just as well in a cold greenhouse or cold frame. Once the plants get their true leaves you can pot them on to their final growing position, which needs to be a fairly large container, or a large grow bag per plant.

Fill 12 inch (30cm) pots with 50% compost and 50% soil and plant the young cucumbers into this. From now on they like high heat and humidity, and some people mulch them with straw. They are ideal plants to grow near a pond or water feature. Keep them well watered and feed them with tomato food at least once a week. You can make a temporary plastic greenhouse around them by pushing canes into the edges of the pot and wrapping cling film around this framework.

You now treat the plant like courgettes, and in June move them to the sunniest spot you can find. Once the fruits are produced, pick them as soon as they are useable. If you let a cucumber mature, the plant will stop production.

Cucumber at a glance

Pot size	Sow/Plant	Care	Harvest
Medium – one per pot	Late April	Feed fortnightly and water frequently. Leave in sunny spot	As soon as they reach a good size

GROWING ENDIVE

There are as many ways of growing endive as there are gardeners. In truth you will have to find the method that suits you. Some sow in small pots indoors in February and transplant these into their final growing positions after hardening off in April. Others sow outdoors in May and then thin them out. The single point is that they do not like being disturbed about the roots, so whatever you do to them, make sure the roots are secure.

I have tended to sow into paper pots in April indoors and then transferred the pots to larger ones, or planters and even hanging baskets of good rich compost in May/June. You can plant them almost anywhere as long as they are not in too windy a position. I treat them as lettuce from then on, feeding them fortnightly with liquid feed and taking leaves as and when I need them.

Endive at a glance

Pot size	Sow/Plant	Care	Harvest
Medium – one per pot	April – indoors	Do not disturb roots. Keep sheltered, feed fortnightly	July–August

GROWING FENNEL

I sow this in an old sink in late May, only a few seeds per sink, then thinning them to two plants per sink. This should give you about one plant every 12 inches (30cm), which is a bit close compared with garden cultivation, but it is quite sufficient for the patio.

They prefer a rich compost with some sand added and need to be fed once a fortnight, watered weekly.

You can snip at the leaves and add them to soups and stews, or even with barbecue meals. When the bulb is about tennis ball size, gather it up for roasting or boiling.

Fennel at a glance

Pot size	Sow/Plant	Care	Harvest
Medium	May – outdoors	Water weekly, feed once a fortnight	Leaves when needed, bulb when 2.5 inches

GROWING GARLIC

Garlic is the most useful plant in the garden, not least of all because of its health benefits and range of uses in cooking. It has been beneficial to humans since the dawn of time because its own immune system actually helps ours. During the First World War the government grew millions of tonnes of garlic to use as an antiseptic in field hospitals. Research stopped into the wonderful properties of garlic when the so-called 'wonder drug' penicillin was discovered, but now it is being looked into again for its anti-bacterial, anti-fungal and anti-viral properties, and it seems to be good for blood pressure too.

Garlic is found in two forms, soft neck and hard neck. Most of what you buy from the supermarket is soft neck, with papery leaves around the central stem. Hard neck varieties have bigger corms, less strong flavour and often small bulbs around the stem.

Soft neck varieties are good for general cooking, but for roasting you cannot beat the hard neck ones, such as *rocambole*, *porcelain* or *purple stripe*. The soft neck varieties come in two forms, silverskin and artichoke. Silverskins are the mainstay of the garlic growing in the garden and they do well in pots. Artichokes have grown out of the desire for having big corms, which in reality is not all that helpful in the kitchen. This trend has culminated in the production of something called 'Elephant garlic' which is actually an imposter. It should really be called 'Garlic flavoured leek'. It is a novelty, but is difficult to grow on the patio and doesn't really do that well in the kitchen either.

Wild garlic, or *Allium ursinum,* is otherwise known of as 'Jack-by-the-hedge'. Jack must have been a rather unwashed chap because you can smell it for miles. It prefers to grow in dark wooded slopes that go down to the river, where the soil is moist. You can buy it these days; but keep it moist. Treat it as the garlic version of chives, chopping the whole plant into things such as omelettes.

It is possible to grow garlic in containers of almost any size. I have grown it in polystyrene drink cups in the past, and it worked too, just giving very small corms! Garlic is best grown in around 6 in (18 cm) pots filled with compost. Keep the pot in a sunny spot, but remember that compost in a pot gets a lot colder than soil in the ground, so protect them in really bad weather with fleece or bubble wrap.

Garlic grows quickly in a good sunny position, but hates to be too damp (except wild garlic) so it is perfect for container growing. Incorporate a handful of sand and another of very well rotted manure into the container to help with drainage and feed the growing plant.

Do not buy supermarket garlic for growing, but make sure you get new stock from a nursery each year. Simply break apart the corms and plant them into the container where they will grow to maturity. It is best to plant garlic in October, to give it a chance to get established before the really cold weather. It likes the cold, but needs to be growing already to get the full benefit of a good freeze. The colder it gets the better the flavour.

From April until June give them a fortnightly feed with a liquid fertiliser and by August the leaves will start to become yellow and fall a little. Empty the pots by hand or if you have grown them in a container, use a trowel.

Fig. 10. Garlic pots

Garlic at a glance

Pot size	Sow/Plant	Care	Harvest
Medium	October–November	Feed fortnightly, check water levels	July

GROWING GOJI BERRIES

Once established, goji berries are incredibly easy to cultivate. Unchecked, they grow into a thick bush that reaches up to 3m tall, with vines that can grow to nearly 4m. If regularly pruned, they will form small, attractive bushes that will produce more berries as a result.

Growing from seed

If growing from seed, use a free-draining potting compost with added vermiculite, that's not too rich in nutrients (as this can make the seedlings grow leggy), and place in a well-lit position with a regular temperature, such as a windowsill (as long as it's not too draughty). Water the compost before sowing the seeds, to avoid them rotting before they germinate. Keep them warm and spray occasionally to keep them moist until they germinate. Once they have germinated and developed around four 'true' leaves, gently transplant them into 3 inch/8cm pots and keep them in a well-lit position indoors for a year, where they should remain warm. The young plants should not be moved outside in their first year as they are not hardy, and are prone to frost damage.

GROWING FROM YOUNG PLANTS

Buying young plants is far easier than growing from seed, as the plants are fully hardy and can be put out as soon as you buy them. Your young bushes will come as bare root plants with no leaves. If planted straight away and watered well they will start to grow leaves within two–three weeks. Place into a 12 inch/30cm pot of good compost. After two years pot in to an 18 inch/45cm pot. Feed fortnightly with liquid fertiliser.

FLOWERS AND FRUIT

After two years the bushes will start to fruit, and from four years you'll start to get very heavy yields. In early summer the bushes will produce small, delicate, trumpet-shaped flowers. Both white and purple blooms can appear on one plant, so they provide visual interest before the berry production begins.

The berries will begin to set in autumn. The ripe fruit are sweet and juicy and almost shiny in appearance. The flowers will continue to bloom right up until the first frosts, however, so your plants will be red, white and purple throughout late summer and autumn.

HARVESTING GOJI

Harvest your goji berries when they are soft, red and glossy looking. Gently twist each berry off the vine, leaving others to ripen. You can eat them fresh, when they're juicy, or dry them. To do this simply place them on a wire rack in full sun, or if that's not possible, place them in a single layer on a baking tray in an oven set to the lowest temperature setting possible. It may take up to 24 hours for the berries to dry; check them regularly, they'll be ready when they are dry and crinkly. They also make a fantastic juice, but it's recommended that you use a juicer for this job as it can be quite tricky otherwise.

Goji at a glance

Pot size	Sow/Plant	Care	Harvest
Large eventually	April	Feed fortnightly	September onwards

GROWING KALE

This brassica has become much more popular recently and rightly so, as kales are very hardy and easy to grow. Another bonus is that pigeons don't seem to like them, so your yield is much higher. You can pick the leaves in their baby stage for salads or leave them to grow to maturity, steaming, boiling or using them in stir-fries.

The very best way to grow kale is to sow from April onwards in 12 inch (30cm) pots or their equivalent. They prefer rich compost with some well-rotted manure and a tablespoon of lime mixed in per pot. Sow thinly and prick out slowly so by June you have only one plant per pot (don't forget you can eat the thinnings).

Water regularly and feed at least once every three weeks. You should stop sowing in August and from this you can get a crop right into winter.

Kale at a glance

Pot size	Sow/Plant	Care	Harvest
Medium	April onwards	Water day, feed every three weeks	From September

GROWING LEEKS

Leeks are not fussy vegetables, but will thrive in a fertile soil which contains plenty of organic matter, so adding compost or well-rotted manure prior to planting is recommended. Leeks grow in a hole in the soil which is filled in by natural watering, but on the patio this needs some attention.

Make a mixture of 50:50 soil and rich compost and fill a sports bag or planter with it. Alternatively, a 12 inch (30cm) pot will do, but the more room you can give them the better.

Leek seeds can be sown under cover indoors in January or February at a temperature of 15°C, in seed trays or module trays about 1–2cm deep. Germination should take between 14–18 days.

Once your leeks are about 20cm tall (this should take 2–3 months), they can be transplanted into their final positions. To a certain degree, the amount of room you can give your leeks will affect their final size. Once all your leeks are in place, water each one in gently. All you need to do now is water the plants regularly and keep them well weeded. An occasional liquid feed through the growing season will help to thicken the stems, but stop feeding in August. In exceptionally dry spells some watering is recommended, but other than that you can just sit back and watch them grow.

Leeks at a glance

Pot size	Sow/Plant	Care	Harvest
Medium – one per pot	January – indoors	Give room, keep weeded and feed occasionally	August

GROWING LETTUCE

Lettuce should be sprinkled all over the patio. Any old spare place you haven't got a plant growing should be filled in with lettuces. You can grow them the whole year round and get a fresh lettuce every single day if you like. Taking December as a starting point, sow them indoors and maintain a temperature of 10°C for them to germinate and grow. You can then put them in a mini greenhouse next to the wall of the house where they will grow happily, but slowly, so long as you protect them from frost. Do this when the plants are as big as your thumb. (You can simply bring them indoors on very cold nights.) Continue to sow indoors until May, when you can start sowing on the patio.

They will grow in any old compost, you can reuse stuff used for a previous crop. When you water them, which should be fairly often, add a dilute (half what the manufacturer states) solution of liquid fertiliser.

Transplanting lettuce is very difficult. The problem is that their leaves grow big but their roots are under-developed and this makes them problem plants to move. The roots get damaged in the process and they wilt off. For this reason they are better grown wherever you start them off.

Simply mark a groove in the soil or compost about 2cm deep and lightly sprinkle the seeds in place with a finger and thumb. Cover and water the young seedlings and protect from slugs as much as you can. As the seedlings grow, thin them by pulling alternate ones out. Use the thinnings in a salad. Make sure they do not dry out, but try to water only the soil and not the leaves, and watch out for greenfly. I usually kill them with my thumb.

From June onwards repeat sowing every two weeks until August when you should stop. Sow a lot in August and you should be able to keep them going until Christmas. The seed packets say stop in July but I never take their advice and have had brilliant crops in November. You can continue their life by popping cut-down plastic lemonade bottles over the pots from September onwards.

Lettuce at a glance

Pot size	Sow/Plant	Care	Harvest
Large 18 inch/45cm – one per pot	April transplant in June	Water and feed regularly	When ripe – late August onwards

GROWING MUSHROOMS

Fungi are nature's decomposers. They take nutrients and energy-rich sugars from dead and dying organic material to make their filaments and reproductive bodies. They number the biggest organisms on the planet, some in America have been shown to spread through the soil over an area of many miles and if you could pull them out of the ground intact would weigh many hundreds of tonnes.

The bits we eat are tiny in comparison with the size of the mushroom, even in patio-grown specimens. Our benefit from fungi is not only from the mushroom but also the fact that mountains of dead things would pile up if there were no fungi to rot them. More interestingly, fungi invade plants and actually help them to grow. In the vegetable garden, all the brassicas do better if they are infected with certain fungi.

But, when you have a plate of bacon and eggs, maybe with a tomato and a fried slice of bread, the thing that makes it perfect (for me at least) is a mushroom.

Sowing whitecap mushrooms in manure

For years, mushroom growers used chicken manure to grow mushrooms in long, dark sheds. You can mimic this process quite easily by using any source of manure – horse is good, or chicken or specially-prepared mixtures along with a mushroom growing kit.

Use a large bucket, or a plastic toy box about 2ft/60cm square. Add the composted material and then sprinkle the spores on top. Water and keep it next to the wall of the house. If you do this in June you will have no problems with temperature. You can expect about 3kg/6½lb of mushrooms that come in waves of around 1kg/2.2lb each time. If you then tip this compost onto the compost heap the mushrooms will come again from the rotting compost!

It can take anything from between a couple of weeks to a couple of months for the mushrooms to appear, largely depending on the temperature. When you first grow mushrooms you begin to wonder if growing food from composted manure can be right. Well, I have tried it in two different ways: the first time I sterilised the compost with a kettle of boiling water; but I also did it without and there was no appreciable difference. As long as you are sure the material is well composted, you should have no problems.

If you prefer, you can get kits that use fresh straw as a basic for growing mushrooms. In this way you will have no issues regarding eating food made from rotting material.

Oyster mushrooms

Oyster mushrooms are easy to grow and can be produced from a bale of straw. Some say to sterilise the straw with boiling water first and then inoculate the straw with the spores. Some people simply fill a bin bag with straw and inoculate this, keeping it warm and moist, so if you have a small greenhouse or cold frame that is easy to keep warm, that's fine.

SHOCKING

After inoculation the oyster mushrooms need to be shocked. This can be either by leaving in the cold outside, or by popping in a fridge if you have opted for a bag (a small bag at that). A few days of cold is all you need then the straw can be left on a tray or a plastic box in a reasonably warm spot – anything over 10°C. Make sure the straw is kept moist and it will take anything up to a couple of weeks to appear. Take the mushrooms when they are young. Once the first bloom of mushrooms has gone away you can get another by re-soaking in cold water and starting again. After the second bloom you can compost the material.

Shiitake mushrooms

I was never really happy with eating something with such a ridiculous name, but it actually roughly translates as tree mushroom. You can buy them as ready-made logs, which you keep as moist and warm as possible – perhaps in the greenhouse or plastic lean-to. Alternatively, you can infect your own logs with little plugs that you push into drilled holes.

The problem with dead wood is that a lot of fungi can break down the lignin in the wood. As this is the basic food source, you need to be sure that your log is fresh and not already infected by stray fungi. Many bracket fungi are poisonous, so you need to be sure you are growing only the right ones.

Choose logs that are about 8 inches/20cm across, birch logs are best, and make them about 3ft/1m long. This type of fungus is applied in little dowels which are already infected with the mycelium. You drill the appropriate holes in the wood to take the dowel and then tap it home. Some kits provide wax to seal the dowels once they have been tapped home. You might get as many as 30 dowels into a log.

The logs should be kept in a shady, moist but not wet area where they can be allowed to decompose. Some people keep them in dustbin bags, some bury them for a while, others simply leave them in a shady area of the patio where little else will grow. It can take up to a year for the log to start decomposing properly.

With all wood-decomposing fungi you have to be sure that you are not going to infect your house, doors or window frames with the spores. Make sure everything is painted properly. In fact there is not much chance of you having problems if you collect the mushrooms reasonably quickly.

GROWING ONIONS

If you are sowing indoors, keep the temperature at around 20°C and use moist compost in plastic modules. The traditional time for sowing onions indoors is Christmas Day, which gives the plants a chance to get established by April so they can be transplanted, but there is plenty of time to get them going in January. The idea is to keep the seedlings warm, well ventilated and then to transplant them to their growing positions in compost that has had a chance to warm up.

The reason for sowing early is that the onion size is directly related to the number of leaves it produces. The more leaves, the larger the onion.

The compost in large containers (I use old washing up bowls or similar sized receptacles) can be heated by bringing it indoors. Prepare by mixing some compost, some ashes if you have them (about 20%) and some sand – a couple of handsful per container. Simply use a pencil to make a hole and then carefully drop the onion in place – firming with the fingers. Keep the plants at around 4–6 inches (10–18cm) apart.

Onion sets

You can buy onions already pre-grown to the size of a button. Simply push them in compost in March or April and leave them to grow. I find it best to use a finger to make a little hole first and then force the little bulb into this. Otherwise, when the bulb bursts into life, the roots push the set out of the pot.

Japanese onions are best bought as sets and planted as above in August. The more the plant produces, the larger the eventual onion. Give them a liquid feed fortnightly and keep watered.

If you plant onions in spring they will be ready in late summer. Much depends on the weather as to their ripeness, too cold and they will be small. Overwintered onions will not keep as well as summer ones because of the ravages of the climate, so try to keep them sheltered if you can.

Leave your onions to bask in the sunshine once you have harvested them. This is a process known as *curing*, in which the outer leaves become leathery and the inner few dry a little, thus protecting the centre.

A note about harvesting onions

I take onions at any stage of their development. Sometimes I take onions and use them as spring onions even though they would bulb up if they were left. The point is that you can change how you think about your produce. Just because an onion hasn't bulbed well (which is sometimes the case growing on the patio) it doesn't mean you cannot chop it up, leaves and all, and use it in your cooking.

Onion at a glance

Pot size	Sow/Plant	Care	Harvest
Large	Late December, early January	Water every other day, feed fornightly	When needed

GROWING PARSNIPS

This plant has to be my one weakness, the aromatic flavour is superb and is enhanced when roasted. The only problem is that it takes a full year for the plant to make the chemicals that give it the distinctive flavour. They are completely hardy and get better as the winter gets colder. You need to give them a good frosting for best results and I have even used the freezer to cool them, but don't tell the wife!

Unfortunately, they are a little like carrots in that stones and excess nitrates make the taproots divide up or grow into strange and impossible shapes.

You can sow parsnips anytime, as long as the pots and containers are not actually freezing. I like to use grow bags that are upturned and have been used once for something else. I do not enrich the compost but choose to feed the plants with liquid fertiliser later in the season. I do add a handful of lime (wear gloves for this) and mix well. Try to sow early in March. Germination takes a long time so be patient and thin out to three plants per grow bag.

They grow slowly, but persevere with them and your patience will be rewarded. Don't be tempted to start them in pots and transplant them – they just end up being all mangled up and grow into grotesque shapes.

Since the parsnip has such a long growing period, it doesn't really matter if you sow some more later in the spring and even in the summer.

Treat the plant as carrots in relation to the carrot fly, which likes parsnips as well as it does carrots.

Water regularly, never let the plant dry out but don't drown them, and feed once every three weeks until the end of September. If you leave them for a week to dry out and then suddenly give them a lot of water, it will make the root split.

Parsnips grow roots one year then seed the next. It is worth keeping a few to grow out because the flower umbrels are glorious to look at, making a great display indoors in a vase. You can keep the seed, too, to plant next season.

Parsnip at a glance

Pot size	Sow/Plant	Care	Harvest
Large	March	Water regularly, feed with liquid feed every three weeks	After one year

GROWING PEAS

You can have more fun growing peas on the patio than any other crop, as they will grow anywhere especially the dwarf varieties. The best thing to do is pop them into a 12 inch (30cm) pot, say six or seven evenly spaced and thin to four plants once they are growing. You can sow every couple of weeks from April right through to August. They do not need particularly rich compost, just enough to get them going. You might provide supports, small sticks or canes will do, then water regularly through the season and feed monthly. The more you feed them the bigger they grow, and you don't really need that on the patio.

You can sow them in a chopped up gutter placed horizontally and filled with compost. Fix this against a wall and in this way have rows of peas at about 2ft high for as long as you wish. They simply grow, flower and finally fruit. April-sown plants will be ready by June/July depending on the weather. Plants sown in August should be in movable pots so you can bring them nearer the warm building or even into a cold frame, and you could have peas, or failing that mange-tout, in October.

Peas at a glance

Pot size	Sow/Plant	Care	Harvest
Small but deep	April	Water regularly, feed once per month	August

GROWING POTATOES

There is nothing so wonderful as emptying your bin of spuds, taking them into the kitchen and cooking them. It is akin to frying your first hen's egg! Potatoes need anything from 12 weeks to 25 weeks to develop, so the sooner you can start them in the early spring the better.

Potatoes come in groups depending on how long they take to grow. First Earlies grow in around 12 weeks, so if you get them in the compost in March they will be ready by the end of May, and what a wonderful first salad they make too! Skin quality is what makes the potato tubers develop and stop swelling, so you can imagine it takes a lot longer for a huge roasting or baking potato to grow than a tiny salad potato.

It is important you grow for the appropriate length of time. Don't try to grow early potatoes for 25 weeks, you will be disappointed. Similarly, maincrop potatoes will not be anything like right to eat as salad potatoes if allowed to grow for only 12 weeks.

Type of potato	When to plant	Cropping
First Earlies	March	12 Weeks 17th March is the traditional time.
Second Earlies	Late March	17 Weeks
Maincrop	Mid-April	20–25 Weeks

How to grow potatoes

Potatoes need lots of organic material in the soil because it is a thirsty plant that prefers to get its water from the soil rather than from the tap. On the allotment the soil is normally enriched with lots of well rotted manure. (Frankly too much is often used!). On the patio make a mixture of 50% compost and 50% well rotted manure (which is even worse than the allotment plot, but needed for growing in containers.) Then add half as much again of soil. This makes for an excellent growing medium for spuds.

Do not save potatoes from last year but buy new 'seed' potatoes each year. Nor should you use potatoes from the supermarket, which often cause the most disappointment. The additional cost of seed potatoes is worth the expense.

CHITTING

This is a mysterious process, a source of a lot of discussion with growers. If you leave the tubers in a light airy position they will change. This change is called chitting. Enzymes inside the tuber will turn the starch into sugar, the tuber will become all soft and springy and as soon as the buds (also referred to as eyes) 'taste' sugar, they burst into life.

Old gardeners used to think the chitting of potatoes gave them a head start, but recent research has shown they do not benefit that much. The truth is that chitted potatoes might not keep so well after harvest and after all, it is a process they will go through under the ground anyway.

PLANTING POTATOES

Method 1: The dustbin Fill a dustbin with compost, made as above, up to ¾ of the height. In this put two potatoes, buried under the surface. Put the lid on. You could also put a door in a wheelie bin as mentioned in Chapter 3.

As the plants grow they will soon appear out of the soil and at the roots tubers will form. These tubers frequently appear at the surface also. Sprinkle compost mixture up around the stems so that the tubers remain snug under the surface. Potatoes exposed to light become green and consequently contain a high level of alkenes, which will at best give you a tummy upset – at worst make you quite ill.

Method 2: Straw You can grow potatoes on the surface by growing in straw. Build a sandpit, soil or compost filled structure about 12in (30 cm) deep. On top of this put a ring of straw around 2ft (60cm) deep and place a seed tuber in the centre. Cover with straw and douse with water. As the potato grows, cover it with more straw and a layer of compost. Build up the straw and compost until the potato plant is looking strong, about two feet high. From then on add compost around the outside of the plant until it becomes impractical. Remember that there is no soil water getting to the plant, so keep a careful eye on the plant in case it starts to wilt, and water if necessary.

Method 3: A plastic bag This works best with Earlies.

This is a fun way of growing spuds. Simply put a tuber in a plastic bag which had a folded bin liner inside it to keep out the light. Then fill with compost and pierce the bag for drainage. You can hang this bag anywhere (I used the washing line once) and you will get a crop if you water and feed regularly. When the plant grows out of the bag, close the neck up a little to keep it under control.

Method 4: A pile of tyres Start with two tyres and place a bin liner in the holes in the centre. Fill this with compost; this is important because there can be dangerous chemicals in the rubber of the tyres which can leach out into your compost. Plant the tuber in the centre and cover, firming down well. Water weekly, but in warm weather you might need to water every other day. As the plant grows taller, add more compost and, when needed, another lined-tyre, to a maximum of four.

Method 5: A rubble bag This is planting the tubers into a rubble bag – a great big bag that is used to deliver stones. Fill it three quarters full with soil and rich rotted manure and plant only three tubers in it – maybe only two. If you use the Pentland series of potato varieties and keep them watered and fed fortnightly with liquid feed, you will get the best part of half a tonne of potatoes in this bag.

Potato care

In the garden soil, potatoes will not need watering unless there is a real drought. Containers are a different matter because there is no soil borne water. Keep your eye on them and only water at the base of the plant. They should never be too wet, and once a fortnight give them a liquid feed. A week before harvesting, in late August or September, you can stop watering them.

Harvesting

Remove the vine and do not compost it before tipping the contents of the container onto newspaper, from which you can pick out the tubers. If you have grown in a big container, watch your back, it can get very heavy! You can lift potatoes with forks, but in containers this is hard to achieve (watch your eyes!). Alternatively you can simply leave them and scrape them out as you need them, having removed the vine beforehand.

Diseases

Potatoes get more diseases than almost anything else in the garden.

Blight – As already discussed, this is devastating and you need to look out for black spots following rain in a hot spell.

Scab – Little brown scabs are no real problem and can be peeled away – don't compost these peelings.

Eelworms – Horrid soupy tubers that sometimes smell are caused by eelworms; microscopic worms that eat away at the potato.

Wireworm – If you grow potatoes in soil that once had grass on it you are likely to get the larva of the click beetle eating into your tubers.

Potatoes at a glance

Pot size	Sow/Plant	Care	Harvest
Extra large	March–April	Water regularly, feed once per month	See previous table

GROWING RADISH

The name 'radish' comes from the Anglo Saxon for red, which is fairly obvious since most of them are red. But you do get green ones and others that are all white. In either case, they will germinate in almost any soil and grow well in almost any temperature. You can sow them in November if you protect them with a cloche. For me, this means growing them in a pot with an upturned cut-down plastic lemonade bottle over them.

Plants grow to around 30cm in height with large, sometimes warty leaves, that are lime green in colour. The older leaves are no good in the kitchen, but are completely wonderful when young. They add quite a kick to salads and if left in the fridge, a crunch too.

The roots obtain their shape quickly, either ball shaped or cylindrical. Ball radishes used to be called summer radish, for no apparent reason because they are just as good grown in spring and autumn.

They grow in cool places that have full sun, which is a bit of a paradox. This makes them an ideal plant for September growing because the days are frequently clear. Their major problem is the speed of growth. If you leave them for a couple of weeks they can quickly become too large and fibrous, making them difficult to pick out of the teeth. The best way of countering this is to sow every two weeks and keep on collecting them once mature.

Sowing in winter

Radishes do well sown in winter, particularly if you can keep them out of the pouring rain. They are fine under a cloche. I grow them in a mini greenhouse to give me a crop in December. You are better growing bolt free varieties ('Boltardy' is one) and give them a frost free spot once germinated. Winter grown radishes have horrible tasting leaves, so don't bother!

Like carrots, make sure your soil is well fed and water retaining, which has plenty of nutrients. As the seeds germinate (you should expect near 100% success) the leaves will peep out of the soil and you can take every other plant in the row to ensure a decent sized crop. Those you have taken to make room for the others can be eaten; they are much too good to waste! Harvest them when the root is an inch or larger in diameter.

Radish at a glance

Pot size	Sow/Plant	Care	Harvest
Medium	From April onwards	Water regularly, feed every three weeks	August onwards

GROWING RHUBARB

Rhubarb is a brilliant grower and will crop for years so long as the compost is free draining. The problem is if it is allowed to stand in water for any length of time it will succumb to fungal infection. The amazing cocktail of flavours comes at the expense of a lot of nutrients – rhubarb is a very hungry plant.

You need an 18in (45cm) pot that is at least 2ft (60cm) deep. Put broken crockery in the bottom and then sand to a depth of 3in (8cm). Mix 50% compost and 50% well-rotted manure and throw a handful of grit in. Each spring, enrich the compost by replacing some of it in the pot with a good few spades of well-rotted manure.

You can grow rhubarb from seed, it is a little time consuming and you have to wait for a crop. In February sow seeds in pots of compost indoors and by May it should have grown into an established plant. Transplant the seedlings to their final containers, which should be a large one around 2ft (60cm) in diameter in late May and keep watered, but not wet.

You are best growing a lot of plants, having them in various containers and not taking too many stalks from each. The following May you may take one or two stalks per plant and then feed with rich compost.

The most common way of obtaining rhubarb is by getting a crown from a friend or garden centre. It is a rhizome obtained by splitting an old plant into many parts. Simply bury the whole thing in compost and wait for it to push through the compost. Treat it exactly as if it were a seedling. It needs a good drink, and that's all.

Rhubarb is an easy-care plant in the soil, more difficult in a pot. The large leaves draw a lot of water and so you have to water it almost daily during the summer. Once a fortnight give it a liquid feed. Large leaves always equate to a thirsty plant, and you should be careful not to let this plant wilt.

Harvest by cutting the stalks at the base, do not pull from a container because you are likely to lift the plant. Take stalks that are an inch thick from April to May, but do not take all the stems, and by the time May has arrived leave the plant alone.

Forcing

Forcing is when you make the stalks grow quickly in the dark. It happens in huge sheds in South Yorkshire, but you can do the same. Place a large ceramic pot over your container and put a pebble over the draining hole because even this small amount of light will spoil the process. The quick growth of the stalks is at the expense of the food resources in the plant. Leaving the plant in the dark for too long will eventually kill it.

New rhubarb takes a good season's growth before it is ready for harvesting but from then on the plant will give plenty of crops year in year out.

Rhubarb at a glance

Pot size	Sow/Plant	Care	Harvest
Extra large	February	Water regularly, feed fortnightly	August

GROWING SAMPHIRE

Salicornia europea is a common plant, growing in estuaries around the world. It has adaptations that allow it to accumulate pure water inside its stems, despite being soaked with saltwater twice a day for many hours. Already under pressure from salty water, the plant can't afford to dry out, so the leaves shrink to small scales to reduce transpiration.

It's a short plant, rarely over 30cm high, with fat, swollen stems that branch in a way reminiscent of other succulent plants such as cacti.

Samphire is said to be so popular just now that half a million servings will be taken over the next 12 months. Our estuaries can't keep pace. Thankfully it's easy to grow. The seeds germinate well in moist compost, best started indoors in spring. The best way to buy samphire is as a plant and pot on to larger growing pots.

It's best to grow this plant in any old compost, in 12 inch/30cm pots. In the wild it grows in all kinds of soils, often muddy. The lack of oxygen at root level is one of the limiting factors to its growth and it should be possible to get specimens at least as good as wild plants because your patio is much kinder than an estuary.

Plant care

Samphire is quite hardy. Remember that in the wild it's covered with cold salty water twice a day, but it's rare that estuaries are frosted. You will need to protect plants from frosts if you want uniformly green shoots. The plant won't be destroyed completely but won't look very appetising after a few nights at −4!

It prefers dampish compost and you'll have to replicate the estuarine environment by watering with salty water! To do this you need 30g of salt per litre of water – try not to use salt that has anti-caking agents in it, and avoid extra-added iodine – and don't let the plants dry out. Feed every six weeks with general-purpose fertiliser liquid.

Harvesting

This is best done as a cut-and-come-again crop. Simply trim off enough stems for a meal and leave the plant alone for a month to recover. With half a dozen plants you should have enough to keep you in samphire as long as you don't eat it all the time!

Samphire at a glance

Pot size	Sow/Plant	Care	Harvest
Medium 12 inch/30cm	March/April	Water with salt water	As needed

GROWING SHALLOTS

In essence, you treat these plants like onions. By far the most common way of growing them is to buy sets and push them into a container, like onion sets. I use ring culture pots, which are designed for growing tomatoes with the hole in the bottom all taped up, around 12 inches (30cm) across and 10 inches (25cm) deep. A single shallot set pushed into a container will give you seven others by the end of the summer.

Make sure they are firmly patted in and not pushed up by their roots. You can plant them any time between February and April and harvest them from July onwards.

Shallots are like small onions and are distinguished by their kick! Pickled shallots are the very best pickles you will find – and go perfectly with the strongest Cheddar cheese and maybe a pint of beer!

Shallots at a glance

Pot size	Sow/Plant	Care	Harvest
Medium	February	Water every other day, feed fortnightly	July

GROWING SPINACH

This is one of those plants you shouldn't over feed. It accumulates nitrates to a dangerous level and consequently I grow it only on spent compost. Spent compost is compost that has been used to grow a previous crop and is therefore lower in nutrients. Apart from that there is nothing to do; it's easy! Simply fill any old container (lots of them) with compost and sprinkle the seeds in. Water and wait. You can thin the seedlings, leaving a single plant per hand-span in large containers, or one plant per 6 inches (15cm) pot. Sow them indoors in December and then outdoors from March/April.

The plants are useable as soon as the leaves appear, but leave to mature – which is about 20 weeks from sowing.

Spinach at a glance

Pot size	Sow/Plant	Care	Harvest
Small	December – indoors	Check water levels	June

GROWING SWEDES

Swedes are wonderful plants; they are packed with sugar yet to taste them you wouldn't imagine so. They are also like a cabbage with a thick root and if you cook a cabbage root you'll see the resemblance.

They grow easily in any kind of compost but in the first weeks they need extra feed. They HATE their roots being messed about with and because of this they are difficult to transplant.

Swedes are longer in the ground than turnips and have a lot of structural tissue to build, so it is no surprise they take longer to mature. In pots they never reach their full potential, and can have a tendency to bolt to seed.

You can grow them in plugs indoors in late March and then plant the whole plug without disturbing the roots into a 12 inch (30cm) pot of compost, enriched with a handful of rotted manure. Do not try to transplant them in any other way, it never works! Feed them fortnightly when watering through the summer. Apart from greenfly and cabbage root fly they do not really have any problems. Harvest them when the roots swell to a ball. It is probably best to take them when they are smaller than you would find in the shops, around the size of a large turnip.

Swede at a glance

Pot size	Sow/Plant	Care	Harvest
Plugs	March	Feed fortnightly through summer	September

GROWING SWEETCORN

Sweetcorn is easy to grow as long as the summer is long and warm, so the cobs can develop. If you can protect your plants from the cold then you are much nearer to getting a decent crop. Once you have got it going, it is fairly easy to grow, even though it can be a little unpredictable.

Plant two seeds in a paper pot in April and thin them to a single plant by removing the slowest growers. The room should be at 20°C and the plants should be reasonably moist but not wet to avoid damping off.

Once they have germinated, keep them a couple of degrees cooler and in a sunny spot as the plants will need lots of light for strong growth.

Planting out is a difficult thing. It needs a deep container for the roots to do well and after a lot of practice, I finally settled on kitchen waste bins. They are expensive to buy, but if you don't mind collecting them from neighbours and so on, you can get a few quite reasonably. Normally the plants need hardening off, but if you plant them so they don't rise above the lip of the container you can cover it with cling film for a few days once they are bedded in.

Plant your sweetcorn in several pots and bunch them together to aid pollination by the wind. Each sweetcorn plant has tassels at the top (the male part) and cobs (female) with 'silks' lower down the stem. Block planting is the best way of obtaining optimum pollination.

They should be grown in a mixture of 50% compost, 20% well-rotted manure and the rest soil with a bit of grit thrown in. Water frequently, feed fortnightly during the summer.

By late summer each of your plants should have one or two cobs. Each cob will have a silk still attached to the top; this will turn dark as the cob ripens. To check for ripeness, pull back a couple of leaves and puncture one of the yellow kernels with your fingernail. If the liquid that is emerges is milky, the cob is ripe.

Sweetcorn at a glance

Pot size	Sow/Plant	Care	Harvest
Medium – very deep	April	Water regularly, feed fortnightly during summer	August

GROWING TOMATOES

Tomatoes are one of those plants everyone should grow. We get all hung up about them needing to be kept hot that we forget that the best tomatoes in the world are grown high in the Italian Alps where the average summertime temperature is fairly cool. Tomatoes grown on the patio are almost always full of flavour, and really exciting for the new grower.

Sow seeds indoors from March to April, but if you are really keen, in February in a propagator at 20°C. Use good quality John Innes 1 compost in modules or seed trays. The ubiquitous drinks cups are superb for the task and I sow 2 seeds per pot. I then prick out the weakest one, unless it looks quite strong, then I use them both.

Transplant the seedlings once they are ready for handling into 8cm (3in) pots. Once the plants have reached a hand-span high you can put them in their final growing positions. If they are going into a mini greenhouse move the pots outside during the day, bringing them back in the evening. This acclimatises them to their new positions. If they are to go outside, take a fortnight over this stage.

If you have room for a larger greenhouse then simply transplant them directly into their final position.

By the end of May, it is time to put the plants into their final growing place. For me this has tended to be grow-bags, spaced 40cm apart and supported from the outset. I use large garden canes firmed deep in the compost. If you have a small greenhouse available, you can plant them in ring culture pots in a bed. I have successfully grown them in the plastic-covered shelving units (three of them along the wall) which hold two plants.

Water the plants well, keeping the compost slightly moist – but do not over water. Too much water at the early stage can promote fungal infections. After a few weeks you will be amazed by the first truss. This is a flowering branch – and once you see this, get watering and feeding. If the weather is hot, water carefully every day; don't splash it about! Add some tomato feed to the water twice a week.

Side shoots

The plant will produce side shoots (branches that come from the leaf nodes of the main vine). Cut these out, mostly as the plant will grow like a bush, increasing the humidity in the plastic covered shelving unit or greenhouse. Humidity means fungal infection, so make sure this is done early.

Keep supporting the plants as they grow by loosely tying them to the cane or support. You will have to decide how many trusses you want from your plants. Three per plant gives bigger tomatoes but you will not get the maximum yield. Four or five is the norm, but you can get as many as seven or eight if you have room to grow such a tall plant. The way to control the number of trusses is to pinch out the highest growing point.

Outdoor tomatoes

I always grow the variety 'Moneymaker' because they do just as well outdoors as indoors. Plant them in 12 inch (30cm) pots (or even 18 inch (45cm)) and put them in the warmest part of the patio from June onwards. They will not grow so large and produce fewer fruits, but are well worth the effort.

Harvesting

Ripening of tomatoes is controlled by the gaseous plant hormone ethylene. This gas is given off by ripe fruit and triggers the ripening process. This is why you sometimes see a ripe banana hanging inside a greenhouse. I never do this because I don't wish to introduce any rotting material into my warm spaces. I prefer to pick any red ones and then, by the end of September, pick the rest and make chutney with the green ones.

Tomatoes at a glance

Pot size	Sow/Plant	Care	Harvest
Growbags	March	Once established, water regularly and add tomato feed twice per week	When ripe – August

GROWING TURNIPS

These are easy and brilliant to grow on the patio. I have a window box which is filled with rich compost and, by the end of March, I have sown a single line of turnip seeds as though they were carrots, about 1 inch (2.5cm) deep. Water them well. Within a week or so they will be pushing through the compost and at this point, thin them out progressively over the next month, so there are plants spaced at 4 inches (10cm). As usual, eat the thinnings. The remaining plants are watered regularly and fed once a fortnight. The turnips are taken when they are tennis ball size.

You can repeatedly sow turnips every couple of weeks until August and still get a brilliant crop in November. The whole year is almost completely punctuated by turnips!

Turnips at a glance

Pot size	Sow/Plant	Care	Harvest
Window box	March	Water regularly, feed once a fortnight	July

CHAPTER 6

HOW TO GROW FRUIT ON THE PATIO

Fruit is the most popular thing to grow on the patio, from a trained cherry tree to a hanging basket filled with strawberries. There is a couple of rules: plant fruit trees when they have no leaves on them, and ensure you get to your fruit before the birds do! There now follows a comprehensive guide to the patio growing of fruit.

GROWING APPLES

You can find an apple to suit you, as there are so many varieties. It is best to plant established trees, as planting pips not only takes years before you get a crop, but also, as all trees are grafted, it is difficult to know what type of fruit you will get in the end. They come in four varieties: cookers, eaters, crab (for making jelly and wine for the brave), and cider apples. Cider apples are medium sweet, cooking apples are less sweet. Crab apples can be very bitter and need a lot of sugar adding to them, but are very rich in pectin for making jelly; and of course, eating apples are completely, deliciously sweet.

Some older varieties are not self-fertile, and you need more than one tree. Modern varieties (those younger than around 80 years old) are self-fertile and therefore perfect for small spaces. You can buy apple trees on dwarfing rootstocks so they fit on the patio easily and they tend to grow very straight. You can also grow them against a wall trained on wires by pruning back growth in the wrong plane.

How to buy apples

Most nurseries sell by mail order and most garden centres keep a reasonable stock of five or six varieties from the same nurseries that you can buy from direct. Look for a sturdy, well-pruned plant that is at least a year old. All, except the most dwarfed trees, will be around four to 5ft tall. In the winter months, from November onwards they will be bare rooted (available to buy with no soil clinging to the roots). In the spring and summer they will be sold in pots. Before you buy by mail order, ask about how they will be delivered, their quality and what special requirements they might have.

Planting

You should plant apple trees when they have no leaves on the branches. Patio apples need a 45cm pot of which the bottom few centimetres are filled with broken crockery for drainage. Use good-quality compost and mix it with ordinary soil. Soil alone will do but is more troublesome to remove in scoops in the spring, when it needs to be replaced with fresh, nutrient-rich compost. Two problems with patio apples (though easily overcome) are first, that they blow over easily (so make sure they are sheltered or tied down) and second, they dry out easily, so water them diligently. Extra watering leaches nutrients so you will have to feed a little more too, around once a month with general purpose liquid feed.

I have two apples planted into a framework that has no bottom, but stands directly on the patio floor. It is around 2ft/60cm deep and is filled with compost.

Care

In the spring, make sure the plant is watered, but don't panic if none of the buds bursts forth until late spring. You may find flowers will drop, fruit may drop, the plant may take a whole year to establish, and there might not be much in the way of fruit for the first three years, but don't panic! If you feed and care for it in the early stages, your apple tree will be fruitful for the next twenty.

Fig. 11. Apple tree

In the spring, take some of the compost away from the top of the plant and replace it with fresh.

Pruning

The pyramid method
The idea with the pyramid method is to make the central stem of the plant lower in height than the lower branches.

- The first thing to do is cut away all dead, broken, or diseased branches. Cut away branches that cross each other or that grow near other branches.

- Find the central branch and prune other branches near to it right to the bottom. Look carefully and cut out the vertical branches, keeping just the horizontal ones and those that, when full of leaves, will cause a lot of shading.

- Take away any branches that come from the base of the plant.

ESPALIER OR WIRE TRAINED

- In your wall, drill two lines of vertical holes at 12 inch (30cm) intervals and screw hoops or hooks into them, through which you fix thick garden wire horizontally. You should have three or four parallel wires.

- Prune the central branch to the level of the top wire and any remaining convenient branches should be moved (trained) to the wires and tied in so that branches are now growing along the length of the wires in a single plane. Remove all the other branches.

- The side shoots will push out lateral spurs which bear fruiting buds. In the winter, the length of the side shoots should be reduced by a third, or to the boundary of your space.

Harvest

It will take three years to get fruit, which will be ripe in October. Cup the apple in your palm and twist it once. If it falls away easily it is ready to take.

JUNE DROP

In June, the tree will shed excess fruit. There is nothing you can do to keep this from happening except making sure you buy dwarf apples for the patio. Once the flowers have set and fallen off, you can spray the plant with an organic insecticide against all sorts of insect pests.

Apples at a glance

Pot size	Sow/Plant	Care	Harvest
Extra large	Mature trees – any time without leaves	Protect from wind, water regularly and feed monthly	September–October

GROWING APRICOTS

Most people think apricots are difficult to grow in the UK, but this is not the case. Biologically they are related to peaches but they don't get peach leaf curl, which makes them even easier to grow outside. As with apples, apricots should be planted as trees.

Apricots are hardy and will grow anywhere in the UK, as long as they can be protected from the very coldest weather. This is particularly important during flowering time, which can coincide with driving snow in some years.

Feeding

Apricots need calcium and so I have always used calcified seaweed as a fertiliser. Grow the plant in a large container (I have used an old-style dustbin in the past), and place it in a position where it can be in full sun, protected from winds. If you are able, a small greenhouse is probably the best place to grow the plant, or even in a conservatory.

Feed in the winter with a mulch made of compost and calcified seaweed at the rate of 5:1 respectively. Then, as the plant grows through the summer, give a general-purpose feed once a month and mulch again in summer. As the fruit is swelling, make sure they do not want for water. The apricots are ripe when they fall off the tree easily.

Pruning

They need only a general pruning to get an open dish shape when the plants are young and then to keep them tidy in following years by taking out crossing branches, as with apples.

Apricots at a glance

Pot size	Sow/Plant	Care	Harvest
Extra large	Mature trees – any time without leaves	Protect from cold, mulch in winter with calcified seaweed, water regularly and feed monthly	August

GROWING BLACKCURRANTS

As with apples, you can find a blackcurrant to suit your environment. There are frost-hardy types as well as plants that do well in any kind of soil. Blackcurrants thrive in an organic-rich soil with reasonable drainage. They prefer full sun but will tolerate dappled shade.

On the patio you need to put them into large containers, at least 2ft (60cm) diameter, and grow the dwarf varieties like 'Ben Sarek'. Mix 50:50 compost and rotted manure. You can plant them in November and any time there are no leaves on the plants.

I cannot stress enough: the bigger the container, the happier the plant will be. But as they are self-fertile, you don't need more than one bush filling the patio.

Care

If, like me, you grow blackcurrants in wheelie bins, you can move them in winter to a warmer spot, but this doesn't have to happen. Sheltering the plant stops them from growing out of the soil and the roots from coming loose in really cold weather.

Once the young fruits are developing, you will need to water regularly and feed every three weeks. They will also need to be protected from birds, who love the fruit, with a covering net. The fruits are ready around a fortnight after they have turned black and can be collected individually or you can wait for clumps. I have to confess that the blackcurrant bush is there for me to get a little treat when I'm working on the patio.

Pruning

Leave the plants for 12 months before pruning, but then remove any stems that are damaged, look diseased or are crossing each other. Then, each winter, prune hard. Do this by opening the centre of the plant by removing a quarter of the central branches. Blackcurrants bear fruit on new wood, so prune away the old wood to encourage growth.

Blackcurrants at a glance

Pot size	Sow/Plant	Care	Harvest
Extra large	Mature trees – any time without leaves	Protect from cold, water regularly and feed every three weeks	Two weeks after colour change

GROWING BLUEBERRIES

Blueberries are fussy plants and in a pot you can pander to their needs easily, probably more easily than in the soil. They prefer acidic conditions and therefore you should provide them with ericaceous compost. Although this is more expensive, it is well worth it. You also need full sun, against a south facing wall is ideal.

You should have two bushes to allow them to cross pollinate, otherwise you will not get much fruit.

When you get your plants put them in 18in (45cm) pots. It doesn't matter what time of the year you do this. Make a compost of 50% ericaceous compost, 40% well-rotted manure and the rest sawdust. (Yes! Sawdust!)

In the first year remove the flowers to allow the plants to grow strong. If you live in a lime area make sure you water only with rain water, and if you cannot do that, a tablespoon of vinegar to a gallon of tap water should do. Feed them every three weeks with liquid fertiliser. In late summer, the fruits will swell and become dark blue, when they are ready for harvest.

Blueberries at a glance

Pot size	Sow/Plant	Care	Harvest
Large	Bushes	Plant in acidic conditions, water regularly and feed every three weeks	August–September

GROWING FIGS

Figs grow on very sturdy bush-type trees, which will pull up your concrete paving or smash down your walls unless you take steps to control them. These Mediterranean plants will quite happily thrive through our winters with little extra care, except sometimes wrapping tender shoots to protect from severe frost.

Strong roots

Figs have roots that will grow through almost anything. It is probably best to keep them under control in a 2ft (60cm) ceramic pot. Possibly the best way to grow them is to make a planter out of paving slabs, cemented together, or large, hollow concrete blocks.

Strong sun

These plants are natives of a thousand miles south of London, hence the more sunlight you can get the better. A wall will retain heat and protect the plant on cold nights, though it is fairly robust and hardy without this. On the very coldest nights, protect delicate fruits with bubble wrap.

Fruit

The flower is never actually seen, being hidden inside the plant and, in the wild, tiny wasps force themselves into the fruit to pollinate it. However, these animals do not exist in the UK, but since it is self fertile, the plant will always set fruit. This happens in the late summer and should be left through the winter to ripen by the following summer. During the winter, remove any inferior or small fruits and discard, to avoid infection and allow the bigger ones to develop.

Care

These are hungry plants and do well with regular additions of good soil-based compost. Fruit plants grown in pots should not be allowed to dry out otherwise fruit will fall. They also do well with a liquid feed (something as simple as tomato food, applied in the usual dose for tomatoes) through the summer. Ensure you get into a routine with watering to get the best results.

Pruning and propagation

Figs fruit on the previous year's wood, so if you cut it all out, you will have no fruit. Take out the most crowded branches in the spring, creating a plant which is open to the air, allowing moisture to be blown away. Prune gently, making sure there are plenty of branches available to bear fruit next year.

Cuttings can be taken off two-year-old wood, which can be then placed into moist compost. On the main plant, remove the shoots that are about 4 inches long, and keep a little of the branch that it came from. They need heat from underneath to root, which should take up to a month, so place them in a 6 inch (15cm) pot of moist compost on a heated propagator.

Figs at a glance

Pot size	Sow/Plant	Care	Harvest
Extra large and very robust. Concrete if possible.	Mature trees any time	Keep watered and protect fruit through winter with bubble wrap	July – one year after fruits first appear

GROWING GOOSEBERRIES

Gooseberries are ideal candidates for a cold patio and if all you have is a few inches of snow and a north facing wall, this plant is for you. It is amazing how well they do in pots as long as you look after them. They have a trick up their sleeves, however; they are at their sweetest a few days after a hot spell, so if you can manage to control yourself, wait a few days before picking them.

They are not too worried about the soil they grow in and you can fill a container with any old compost. Drainage is the important part – fill the bottom of the pot with crocks to improve the drainage. To grow gooseberries in a pot you must make sure they won't ever be standing in water and so you need a good 12in (30cm) pot. Fill the bottom with crocks and then a layer of grit. Plant the specimen in compost on top of this.

Plant bushes in October when there is still a little warmth in the air and your plant will settle down in the pot. Put the plant against the wall of the house for a little extra warmth. In February prune the plant quite heavily (see below) and then add a layer of good quality rich compost on top of the old stuff. Each year you should replace as much compost as you can with fresh in the autumn and add a good handful of slow release fertiliser.

As long as the plant has fruit, give it plenty of water. Once a month give a little liquid feed in the water too. But in all things, the mantra 'drainage is the key' is important.

Pruning

They are so full of sugar that gooseberries are prone to fungal diseases. They also grow with a lot of crossed branches. The problem is that when the fruits form they rot because the humidity around the branches is so high. This is alleviated by cutting away the branches to let the air circulate. As in most pruning you are looking for an open dish shape.

Prune in February when the plant has no leaves on it and you can see the thorns! Remove dead wood and then have a look for any crowded branches. Cut out all the branches that cross over one another. There is nothing difficult about it, just cut away, but wear gloves unless you have elephant skin.

In May you will begin to see how much fruit is developing and take out smaller fruits to allow air to circulate around the rest. This way you will have no problems with botrytis. You also get bigger, fuller, sweeter fruits this way.

After a year, pot the whole plant on to the next size up, and repeat this process every year until the plant (or yourself) is old and gnarled.

Gooseberries at a glance

Pot size	Sow/Plant	Care	Harvest
Large	Plant bushes in October	Ensure plant is open by pruning, keep watered, but drained. Feed using slow-release fertiliser	July

GROWING GRAPES

Grapes were brought to this country by the Romans and in one form or another have remained here for 2000 years. Why we think them difficult and that they can only be grown in hot climates is probably more to do with wine companies than anything else. Grapes like hot summers, dry springs and cold winters. That could be the UK to a 'T'.

All you need to know about grapes:

1. They don't fruit on new growth.

2. They don't like to be cut when there are leaves on the vine.

3. Fruit rots easily, like gooseberries.

4. They need a sleep in the winter (so keep them cool).

5. New vines take 3 years to produce fruit.

There is a lot said about pruning regimes. All you have to remember is that you cut in winter and that you have some vines that will grow this year and only have leaves, but next year will also bear fruit. If you don't prune at all you end up with a long straggly plant that grows for ever and doesn't produce that much fruit.

The ideal spot

I took the roof off my car port and replaced it with corrugated clear plastic sheeting. An old tub, about 3ft (1m) diameter and about the same high, houses my grape vine and it trails along under the sheeting. In the winter the wind howls through the car port and the vine loves it.

Training systems

There are a number of culture systems based on making either a single stem (cordon) or a double one. The vines are either trained on a horizontal parallel wire system, so that the wires are at heights of 12in (30cm) to support the cordons, or a single wire on a frame or around the wall of the house (or hanging from the carport as in my case).

SINGLE CORDON VINES

The traditional way to grow vines in the UK is to plant them outside a polytunnel and train the vines through the plastic (or a hole in the greenhouse glass) to the inside. You can do the same on the patio, by leaving the branches outside, especially if you have somewhere warm for the summertime plant to grow, which usually means by the house. Build a wire frame, much as you did for apples, to aid this.

The pot should be filled with rich compost, mixed with plenty of well-rotted manure. Traditionally vines were planted above a rotting dead sheep. In the summer of the first year allow the plant to grow, and pinch back any lateral shoots to around five leaves.

When the leaves have fallen off in the winter, cut back the main shoot by just over half and cut the laterals to a single bud each.

The following summer treat the plant like you did the previous summer; tie in the main shoot and build your frame of wires. Take out any flowers that form.

The following winter cut the main shoot back to old wood and the laterals to a strong bud each.

In effect, you have strengthened and prepared your plant ready for producing laterals that you will now tie in the following spring and summer. The buds will then grow out, and the resulting growth is trained along the wires.

The third summer allow one bunch of grapes per lateral shoot to form, and any sub-laterals that form keep to a single leaf. In the winter, when the grapes are taken and the leaves have fallen, cut the laterals to two buds. It is these buds you will use next year and so on.

Fig. 12. Vine

Care

Indoor vines do well if they are fed with tomato fertiliser each month. Do this a couple of weeks after they have burst into life in the spring, until the grapes are ready for picking. Water diligently, but ensure the humidity is low around the leaves and fruit.

Harvest

Just like gooseberries you have to watch for ventilation because of the high sugar content. This means removing fruits and increasing ventilation. If you are growing with tomatoes in a greenhouse be careful about watering because the toms evaporate a lot of moisture. Try not to do this.

When collecting grapes, cut at the piece of vine they are joined onto and don't handle the fruit at all because you might spread fungal spores around the plant.

If you are growing outside you will rarely be troubled with botrytis but a monthly spray with Bordeaux Mixture (which was invented by Benedictine monks just for this purpose) will keep problems at bay.

Grapes at a glance

Pot size	Sow/Plant	Care	Harvest
Extra large	Vines in May	Protect from humidity, water frequently and feed once per month	August

GROWING KIWIS

The kiwi came to our shores from New Zealand, where much of the climate is not dissimilar to our own, so you would have thought it possible to grow the plant here in the UK. There have been a couple of problems growing kiwis whose varieties have been made up of male and female plants. I have always found the male one in particular has lacked vigour and didn't always do too well. This would leave me with masses of luxurious growth on the female plant but no fruit.

Furthermore, older varieties need quite a lot of sunlight to successfully set fruit and this has restricted their popularity, though examples of good fruiting as far north as Yorkshire do exist.

Easy grow patio version

With the introduction of the variety 'Jenny', kiwis are easy to grow. It's getting them to bear fruit that is the problem. Fruit is produced on new growth that appears from canes that are a year old and older. The amount of fruit each bears diminishes each year, the older the cane, proportionately, the less fruit they bear. Cut out the canes once they are three years old, down to their base. Maintain a healthy number of new, one- and two-year-old canes and you should have good fruiting.

'Jenny' is a self-fertile variety that is bought as a young plant, taking away the problems of pollination. The plant is hardier and will fruit in more temperate climates. You can train the canes (some people call them vines) on a series of wires attached to a southern-facing wall or trellis.

You will buy 'Jenny' as a pot plant around 3ft tall, and it will be in its second year. This plant will take another two years to start producing fruit, and should not be pruned until then. Choose a sunny aspect and provide a rich compost. Once the plant has been set in its final place, give it a good watering and then leave it for a couple of weeks before assessing the need for another drink. They usually do not require much in the way of watering unless there has been a considerable drought.

Put the plant into the largest container you can find – I use an old wash tub with a diameter of around 3ft (1m) and a similar depth. Possibly the most useful and accessible container for this plant is a plastic water butt and I have seen them in such containers that have been sawn two thirds of the way up leaving one container for the kiwi, and another for whatever else you need.

After the plant has fruited, prune to the oldest canes, but only one or two, and train the younger ones. Once your plant grows it will reach a peak of production at around six to eight years. By this time you will have a well-developed regime of pruning and fruiting.

Prune in February and, each April, give the plant a good dressing of well-rotted compost and some organic fertiliser. Scrape away at the old compost and replace it with fresh as far as you are able. The plant is quite hardy in the winter, just do not water unless it is showing signs of stress. During the summer, feed the plant with a good liquid fertiliser (I use tomato feed) through the flowering and fruit-setting period, once a month until September.

Grow from cuttings

You can take cuttings of old stems in summer, as long as you include the growing point – the tip of the plant. They are placed into moist sand or a combination of sand and compost. They will strike in the autumn and by the following spring can be potted up as individuals. These can then be allowed to grow during the whole of the following year and put into their final positions in the following spring. I have found that the plant is so vigorous that two plants is one too many.

Harvesting

The fruit starts to appear as small green berries that grow to plum size. They change colour from green to brown once ripe. When this colour change is just underway, you can pick them. They are usually hard and take a couple of weeks to soften ready for eating. They will keep all year in the fridge and a couple of months on the table. If you pick them too early they will be tart and have no sweetness, but if you pick them too late they will shortly turn into a mushy mess.

The fruit of the self-fertile varieties are on the small size compared with the commercial ones, and they are less hairy. Some people say that if you can cross pollinate a self-fertile variety, the fruits are bigger, but I haven't found anyone that has really done it.

Disease

There are few problems with kiwis in the UK. They can, if over watered a great deal and the soil is poorly drained, get root rot, but this is quite a rare problem. Similarly, red spider mite can create a problem, particularly if it is in a small polytunnel, but this too is uncommon. One of the strangest problems reported about kiwi plants is that some cats like them so much they dig and claw at the base of the stems.

Kiwis at a glance

Pot size	Sow/Plant	Care	Harvest
At least 1m	Mature trees – any time without leaves	Feed monthly in summer, water only when needed.	Just as fruit change colour

GROWING MELONS

To grow melons on the patio requires a little skill and a lot of perseverance. They are grown normally on little mountains of soil where they can bask in the sun, but the patio cannot easily produce this. But you can keep them clean by allowing them to lollop over the side of the pot. You are best starting them indoors, sowing two seeds vertically in a 3in (8cm) pot of good John Innes No. 1 compost.

Transplant outdoors in June. Put it in an 18in (45cm) pot of very rich compost. Wrap the pot in black plastic to help it warm up and keep the plant in the hottest part of the patio.

When you take the melon outdoors try to cover with a cloche for as long as you can. I have made a little tent in the past from clear plastic that fits over the plant when the weather is poor. Melons need heat and good sunlight.

All this talk of global warming is good for melons because they like the weather hot, but along with the heat we seem to get our fair share of wind and rain, which they hate. We have enough heat, but make sure they are in a well protected sunny spot. Driving windy rain is a real problem for melons, they'll get rot type diseases, they will be smaller and they will have no flavour.

Don't let the plant dry out. I have found that the best approach is to water every three days and every second watering to give the plant a feed with tomato fertiliser. When the melons are swelling out you can water every two days, remember little and often is best. Make sure that long periods of drought followed by emergency watering never happen.

Pollinate the plants by hand as the female flowers appear. Again I keep three good ones rather than a lot of small ones per plant.

Harvesting

When harvesting, melons simply slip off the vine if you move the plant around. When you have taken them, a period in storage of about a week will improve their sweetness. Some melons, the Persian types, remain fixed to the vine and you have to cut them off. These do not improve much in storage at all. A sure sign of ripeness for harvest is the aroma of wonderful sweetness which is given off by the fruits to attract someone (or some animal) to come along and eat it.

Problems and diseases

In the UK melons suffer from people over-watering them, from cool conditions – especially late frosts, and over-feeding. When this happens they will become too fleshy.

Melons have large watery cells but unlike citrus fruits they do not have much natural antifreeze. As the cells cook they break apart, spilling their contents inside the fruit and this then encourages fungal growth. The plant can cope with a small amount of such damage but as soon as a certain level is reached, the plant goes into rapid decline. Also the cells that are broken invariably contain enzymes that work on the rest of the tissues, causing more damage.

The most common problems are powdery mildew and root rot. The sugary fruits are the major target for fungal problems. You can use a copper based fungicide once a month but they seldom do much good. The key to success is care. Keep the plant free from drought, free from being waterlogged, at an even temperature and do not use anything other than good quality, well-rotted compost. If you feel you are not doing so well, keep only one fruit per plant and have it as a very expensive luxury.

Melons at a glance

Pot size	Sow/Plant	Care	Harvest
Large	Seeds in April	Protect from weather, water every other day (every day in hot weather), feed every third day watering	When fallen from vine

GROWING PEACHES

Peaches need warmth and are difficult to grow on the patio unless you have a greenhouse to move them into whenever it is too cold. Pot-grown trees produce lower yields but can be moved around as necessary and even brought outside on warm sunny days. Fan training is the traditional method of growing peaches, as the height can be easily restricted. However, you cannot fan train a peach and move it around at the same time.

You can provide adequate support by using horizontal wires attached to upright posts, but bear in mind eventual spread can be up to 12ft.

Fruiting begins when the trees are four years old, and they can produce crops for up to 30 years. Peaches and nectarines fruit on young shoots, so after harvest cut back all the branches that have fruited to a point where a new shoot has appeared.

The only way I have seen peaches doing well on a patio, and I have never had room to do this myself, is when planted in a space left by a paving slab removed from the patio and trained against a southern wall.

PEACHES AT A GLANCE

Pot size	Sow/Plant	Care	Harvest
Extra large	Mature trees – any time without leaves	Keep warm and water at soil	July

GROWING PEARS

In essence, there is no difference between apples and pears. Growing apples and pears in pots is very common, as long as you protect them from the worst of the weather. Pears especially don't like driving winds. You will have more control over drainage in the pot, but you will have to water your tree every day over the summer. They will also need feeding regularly.

Containers should be as big as possible with a minimum depth of 18–24 inches (45–60cm). Fill the bottom with crocks and then a few inches of grit on top of this to help drainage. Make your compost out of one third soil, one third compost, and one third well-rotted manure.

Water the pear when the compost feels dryish, but don't let it completely dry out. Feed once a month with liquid fertiliser. Mulch with fresh compost in spring and summer. In the winter, when the tree is dormant, scrape as much compost out as you can and renew.

Pruning a bush pear

Year 1	To prune a new tree, count four buds from the base of the tree and cut the main stem about 1–2 inches (2–4cm) above this bud.

| Year 2 | From now on all pruning takes place in the winter, no later than the end of January. Cut all the side branches back by a third of their length. |

| Year 3 | From now on, every year, cut back the new growth by a third. Do not cut the old wood unless it is diseased. You are trying to keep the mass of branches light. Always cut just above an outwardly facing bud then the tree will branch outward. |

Pears at a glance

Pot size	Sow/Plant	Care	Harvest
Extra large	Mature trees – any time without leaves	Protect from wind, water regularly and feed monthly	September–October

GROWING PINEAPPLES

It is possible to grow pineapples from shop-bought fruits, by planting the crown (leaves on top). However, some supermarkets pull out the growing point of the pineapple, thus increasing its shelf life. No amount of potting and watering will make these crowns grow. Choose a plant that is completely intact with leaves on the top. Of course make sure the fruit is edible because we do not need this part for the growing process, so you might as well enjoy it.

Removing the crown

You are looking to find the growing buds inside the leaves of the pineapple. Some people slice the top off the pineapple, with a little bit of flesh behind it. Others twist the top off the plant and throw it away. This is the part you need if you want the novelty of growing your own pineapples. Once you have your top, leave it to dry out for a while on a shelf. When I first did this I placed it in water and the plant rotted very quickly. If your plant shows any sign of rot you should discard it straight away – pineapples are susceptible to fungal infections.

Rooting

If you peel away at the leaves you will find some little rootlets, and it is these that are going to grow. The embryonic roots need to be coaxed into life, which is done by standing them in moist compost. You can do this is two ways; cut out a root with a little of the stem, or simply place the whole piece in compost. The best way is to put the whole piece of pineapple in an 8in (20cm) pot of moist compost. Keep the compost moist and simply leave it. It might take months for the plant to grow but eventually the roots will take off.

Dead leaves

The old leaves of the pineapple, if you have any remaining at all, will die back and you should remove them. If you look closely, you will see the replacements beginning to form.

Re-pot the plant after a year into a 10in (25cm) pot, and it should go into an 18in (45cm) one the year after.

Care

Sparingly water your plant so the compost is lightly damp and, during the summer, feed with an all-purpose fertiliser once a month. Keep it free from frost at all times, but you can take it outdoors in the summer. Keep the minimum temperature to 13°C.

Flowering

After a couple of years the plant will send out a flower like a bromeliad, of which family pineapples are members. You can speed up the flowering by using the plant hormone ethylene, released by other ripe fruit. So if you put the plant next to the fruit bowl you will have greater success.

Pineapples are a bit of fun more than anything else, but when you get a successful fruit it really brings a smile to your face.

Pineapples at a glance

Pot size	Sow/Plant	Care	Harvest
Medium – repotting later	Crowns inside	Water sparingly and feed monthly	After 2½ years

GROWING RASPBERRIES

There's a funny saying about raspberries: 'They are thirsty plants that like dry feet', which sounds like a contradiction, but is true. They prefer free-draining soils that have plenty of moisture available, but they rot if there's any standing water, which makes them great for growing on the patio. They are woodland plants so shade isn't a particular problem, but they do much better in full sun.

Summer-fruiting raspberries

These are planted in a box (if you can manage it) 18 inches (45cm) deep, 20 inches (50cm) wide and as long as you need. The box is filled with good quality compost and well-rotted manure, with plenty of grit and crockery for drainage. This is done during the winter.

Running horizontally down the middle of the box, fix a wire to canes on either side for them to be supported. The raspberries should be planted at intervals of 18 inches (45cm) and well firmed-in. Pile a little more compost over the base of the plants so that it comes close to the top of the box.

New raspberry bushes, once planted, should be cut down to 8 inches/20cm from the soil. Without this they never seem to grow vigorously at all. If any fruit appear in the first year, pull them off and allow all the plant's resources to go into making good roots and healthy crowns (the complex system of stems below the surface). As the plants grow they'll need to be supported on the wires.

In the second year, feed them in the late spring with an organic fertiliser. A handful of bonemeal for every two plants, forked in with a little compost is a good idea. The raspberry canes will grow and fruit. In July, or once the harvest has been taken, cut the old canes down to 6 inches (15cm). Any non-fruiting canes should be tied-in and allowed to grow.

Autumn-fruiting raspberries

These are grown singly as standalone plants and they need no support. You should grow them in large pots, at least 18in (45cm) with good quality John Innes No. 3 compost. Make sure they are well firmed in and they are deeply set in the compost. You should plant in October and put them in a sheltered part of the patio.

Summer fruiting raspberries are pruned at the end of the summer; autumn fruiting ones are pruned in winter. All you do is cut the growth back to 6in (15cm) and the new growth will provide the later season's berries.

Care of raspberries

Raspberries need water and in order to get good fruit you should water regularly. Raspberries are mostly water so it's logical really. As with many plants on the patio, you need to protect them from the effects of water too. During dry periods give them a really good soaking once a week. Every two years, in the winter, lift them out and replace the compost as best as you can, with rich manure-filled compost mixture.

Raspberries at a glance

Variety	Pot size	Sow/Plant	Care	Harvest
Summer-fruiting	Extra large – wide box	December–February	Cut down when planted, water regularly but ensure drainage. Replace compost every two years.	July–August
Autumn-fruiting	Extra large – wide box	October	Prune back in February, water regularly but check drainage. Replace compost every two years	October

GROWING STRAWBERRIES

The only time you have to worry about strawberries is if you have new growth in a frosty spring. Every other possible combination of weather conditions and plant type does not matter. They are very hardy and will easily live through the worst winters. In the spring, I cover them with fleece if the weather is very poor.

They prefer (though it is not essential) a well drained position, so put plenty of grit underneath them. The basic job of a strawberry is to turn sunshine into lovely flavoured, sweet juice. So the more sunshine they get, the better. Originally, the plant was native of the woodland edge, but just as poor, modern dairy cows have become milk-generating machines, modern strawberries are sugar factories. So get them into the sun!

Planting

Strawberries are seldom, if ever, sold as seed, but as new plants. They are best planted in April and May, though any time except the winter or a frosty spring is fine. Plants bought in September also do well, getting through the winter with no real problems.

Grow them in pots of all sizes and you can also buy strawberry planters. A good handful of grit in the bottom increases the drainage and prolongs the summertime growth if it's rainy. Then in May, lay straw under the leaves and developing fruit so that none is resting on the soil.

Plant the strawberries so that the crown in the centre of the plant is at the soil's surface. Too deep and they will be susceptible to rot, too shallow and they will refuse to grow at all. The plants need to be watered every couple of days when first planted, but after that weekly should be fine unless there are some serious droughts.

Strawberries have problems with greenfly; I usually use my finger to remove them. Take care with their removal as the greenfly can carry viruses from which the strawberries can really suffer.

A plant takes a year to become well established. In its second year, it is in full production, in its third year it begins to succumb, and in its fourth year it is not worth keeping. So every third year it is best to replace your strawberry plants. This is done by using the plant's own system for dealing with this problem: runners.

Runners

Strawberries send out sideways branches called runners, which at intervals of about 12in (30 cm) give little plantlets. These are genetically identical to the parent plant so produce exactly the same fruit. When the plant is a year old these runners should be cut off to allow the plant to grow strong. In the second year put the plantlet into a 3in (8cm) pot and place a pebble on the runner to hold it down. After a few months the runner will have rotted away and you have a new strawberry plant. This plant does not suffer from the viruses of its parent and is essentially a brand new plant. It will though inevitably start to have problems over time, in the same way as its parent.

Your replacement plants can be kept in a cool greenhouse in their little pots over the winter and planted out into larger ones in the spring. You need to acclimatise them to the outdoor life by taking them out during the day and bringing them in at night. These plants are so tough that you can ignore them and they will still grow, even though they look half-dead.

Strawberries at a glance

Pot size	Sow/Plant	Care	Harvest
Medium	April–May	Protect from frosts in spring, water weekly	When berries are red – July/August

GROWING CITRUS PLANTS ON THE PATIO

If you have a conservatory, it is possible to grow your own citrus plants. They have been grown for many hundreds of years and it is quite possible for you to mimic the environment needed to grow such exotic plants.

The plants in this section; oranges, limes, lemons, grapefruits, kumquats etc. are easily grown and are prized for their flavour and the supposed Vitamin C content. In truth the most important natural source of Vitamin C is the rosehip, but when the British navy finally accepted the link between Vitamin C and scurvy they loaded their ships with the fruit, and the idea has stuck in the nation's imagination that lemons are full of Vitamins, which they are in a modest way. Indoors in the UK it is possible to grow a very wide variety of citrus fruit, not just the basic oranges and lemons.

Conditions for growth

The big problem is the need for a frost free environment in the winter months. Cold, driving rain will kill them off, and so they should have the protection of a cool greenhouse or conservatory. If the temperature drops much below 3°C they will really suffer. They need a sunny spot too, not for the warmth it brings, but they need lots of sunlight. They can be brought outdoors in the summer, and the old English 'Orangery' always had extra wide doors for this purpose.

During the winter they need less water, but they also have a tendency to flower during this period. I have always wanted an orange in flower on Christmas Day, but have never quite managed it so far.

You need a large terracotta pot as it is porous and provides an amount of air to the roots. You should not use plastic pots because the roots can starve of air. Start with a 2ft (60cm) pot when you first buy your tree and each year pot it on until the plant is living in a 3ft (1m) pot. Clearly this is too heavy to move around at this stage, so it may as well be treated as though it was a permanent house plant.

Fill it with soil-based compost (John Innes No. 3) and incorporate up to 15% sand into the mix. They don't like to be too wet, but because they are grown in pots they need a lot of moisture in small amounts. It is the old conundrum the patio gardener has to live with: the need for water without water-logging the plant.

Use a good quality general fertiliser at least once a month during the summer and once a fortnight in the spring. You can buy special winter feed for citrus plants, with a slightly different balance of nutrients, but unless you are going to show the fruit in competitions, this is an unnecessary expense.

Propagation

It is great fun to open a lemon or an orange and try to germinate the seed. This is quite possible in most cases and the plant will grow readily. It will take a full decade before the plant will flower, however, and you might not wish to wait that long. You can also take cuttings in the autumn. Simply take off pieces of branch that have two buds on it and pop them into moist compost. Around half of them will take and you can pot these on as soon as they have rooted.

As with apples and other top fruit, citrus trees bought from garden centres and nurseries are grafted onto different rootstocks. You should try to get a dwarfing rootstock, ask the nurseryman for his help.

Re-potting and pruning

Pruning takes place in the spring when you are trying to make a pleasing shape with no criss-crossed branches. Trim just above a fat bud and do so that if the rain were to fall on the wound, the water will fall away from the bud. You can trim to suit the size of the room with no problems.

Pests and problems

All the family suffer from the same set of pests from aphids, to red spider mite and scale insects, which are probably the worst. The way to tell a healthy plant is by seeing the leaf drop in winter. They should only lose around a third of their leaves and no more. If they lose more, re-pot the plant and give it a little water.

Yellowing leaves is a sign of stress; too much water, too little water, too cold or too dark.

Keep plants well ventilated but out of strong draughts to avoid botrytis and other fungal infections.

Keep them watered little and often, but avoid them standing in water on the patio. You can lose them in August if there are flash floods and you are unable to get them out of the water, perhaps because you are on holiday. Don't be tempted to bring the plant indoors too soon, make a polystyrene cape for it and keep it outside until late September if there are no frosts.

Oranges

Oranges came to the UK with the slave trade when botany was the national craze. Navel oranges came from a single mutant orange found in Brazil and have a double flower; so there is always a 'baby' fruit inside. You can buy oranges for growth in the UK where blanco oranges are the favourite. They are smaller and so can be borne on smaller trees. Most fruits can be harvested from November to December.

Grapefruit

Grapefruits were also brought here from the West Indies. They came from a mutation from oranges and were grown out at Kew and private gardens. These are easiest to grow and can be treated like oranges.

Kumquats

Kumquats are fast growing. They can be eaten complete and are great for making a soaked fruit in syrup. They are best not moved around.

Clementines and Satsumas

These plants are brilliant at Christmas and when they are grown at home they ripen just around Christmas too. An annual trimming keeps them in check and they have brilliant flavour. To my mind there is no better Christmas present.

Limes and limequats

Limes can be trimmed to about 5 ft high and then will remain happily producing fruit each year for many years. There are half a dozen varieties that grow well in the UK, some turning yellow, others remaining acid green in colour. A limequat is a cross between a lime and a kumquat. You can eat the whole fruit and it tastes like a lime.

CHAPTER 7

HOW TO GROW HERBS ON THE PATIO

The fact that we call some plants vegetables or others fruits, does not detract from the fact that in a very real way all plants are actually herbs. Their use in the kitchen and in medicine or around the home is just as important today as ever in the past, and in a time of fast food perhaps we need to take a step back and renew our long-treasured relationship with British herbs.

There is a long list of plants that we have gathered together with the general umbrella title 'herbs'. Their origins often reach into the distant past, long before fast food or kitchens even, and many of them, like garlic, have been helping the human immune system deal with invaders for thousands of years.

The reasons for using herbs have not changed over the years, although we probably know less about them now than we ever did. Of course, flavour is an important consideration but they are also used medicinally, such as feverfew or comfrey; or cosmetically such as eyebright, rosemary or violets. Sometimes they are used purely for colour such as angelica, and other times they are the main part of the dish – often the case with chives or parsley.

The Romans introduced many herbs into the UK. They decorated their heroes with herbs and used various plants as disinfectants (as did the Greeks); and many more modern uses for herbs, such as placing them with linen sheets, pot pourri, and window bouquets, reflect this ancient use. Many herbs were afforded magical properties which, because of their ancient medical use, have come into modern folklore. For example, elderberry, because of its sedative qualities, has the reputation of carrying anyone who takes it, or even sleeps under the tree, into the fairy world.

CHOOSING AND GROWING

Fresh is best! But sometimes fresh can be a little disappointing, especially when you buy those little tubs of living herbs from the supermarket. To get the best from them you need to transplant the herb into some rich compost, place it in good strong sunlight and feed it with a solution of fertiliser. After about a week you will really see the difference. The colour, fragrance and taste will be so much better.

Most herbs do well in pots of compost. Rapidly growing plants, such as mint, should be grown only in a pot because otherwise it takes over the garden. Most of the flavours of herbs develop when the plant is well fed and not under water stress. On the whole, herbs are easy to grow. It is perhaps best to earmark a really sunny spot, near the house, and remember to water them every day during the summer or warm weather.

One of the fine jobs of autumn is to dry your herbs for the winter. Alternatively, you can freeze them in closed food bags. Preserving herbs in such a way as to preserve the essential oils inside them is quite an art and it is possible to get well preserved or dried herbs – especially if you have done it yourself! Sometimes drying concentrates the flavour, and so you need to modify your quantities.

GROWING HERBS

The following section discusses how you can grow a variety of herbs in a small space.

GROWING ANISE

Anise is an ancient plant used from before the golden age of Ancient Greece. It is aniseed in flavour and you can use the seeds and the leaves.

Sow a few seeds in a large pot, at least 18 inches (45cm) in April, and fill it with compost made from 25% sand, the rest compost and a handful of grit. Let it flower in the following year and it will produce loads of strongly flavoured seeds. Take off the seed heads and store in paper bags until they burst, then remove to airtight containers.

GROWING BASIL

This is one of those plants you should grow in pots and containers wherever you have space. It is filled with aroma and makes the patio in high summer so fragrant. Basil is a health-giving plant and grows fairly easily as long as it has plenty of sun.

In the spring, sow seeds in compost and keep it frost-free. I sow them in April, in any old container as varied as old boots to old tomato tins as well as more conventional pots and planters. Try to keep the plant in a constant temperature, around 15C but not below 10C. The seedlings will emerge after a fortnight.

It needs little care, just make sure it never dries out by watering from below and feed it with liquid fertiliser once a fortnight to make sure you have the most aromatic leaves. If flowers appear, pinch them out to encourage more leaf growth.

By late autumn I bring a few pots into my plastic patio greenhouse and keep them going as long as I can into winter. The rest I take up and compost, starting again the following spring.

GROWING BORAGE

You can sow borage in pots or trays indoors in March. It needs pricking out into 3 inch (8cm) pots and then potting on to until you get to 12 inch (30cm) pots. It is not that

Fig. 13. Basil

bothered about the compost and you can use old compost from last year. Keep the plants watered regularly and feed fortnightly.

You can take the flowers to flavour drinks and it is a major constituent in Pimms.

GROWING BURNET

This plant is used in teas and is supposed to help with blood flow and circulation, but don't take my word for it and never treat yourself for medical conditions. Burnet grows very easily in pots of compost with grit in it to aid drainage. Sow indoors in March and move it outdoors at the end of April. You need ordinary compost and a 12 inch (30cm) pot. I sow a few seeds and thin them so I eventually have a single large plant. You simply take the leaves when you want them.

To make a tea simply put a few leaves in the bottom of a cup and pour on boiling water.

GROWING CARAWAY

This plant, related to the carrot, can be eaten from the roots to the seeds, though it is the seeds that are mostly used now. Sow a few in 12 inch (30cm) pots in September.

Keep them indoors and frost-free during the winter and you will have decent plants by April. Thin them out to one per pot. You can transplant the thinnings to other 12 inch (30cm) pots. In the first year, the plant grows about a foot high. Keep it watered and fed fortnightly.

Bring it near the house for protection in the second winter, and the following spring repeat the care regime until the plant sets seed. It will double in height too. Collect the seeds.

GROWING CATNIP

This is a type of mint highly enamoured by cats, but it looks very beautiful and is worth growing. It is perennial but I find on the patio all the nepetia species, of which catnip is a variety, do well as bedding plants. Simply sow in March indoors into ordinary compost and prick the seeds out into 3 inch (8cm) pots.

It grows quite large, and in June I transplant it to 12 inch (30cm) pots.

Fig. 14. Catnip

GROWING CHAMOMILE

This is a long-loved plant of the English garden. Arthemis, or chamomile will grow all over the patio if you let it. I like to sprinkle seeds around large planters, cracks in paving stones, anywhere there is a bit of earth for it to grab a hold on. You get bright green leaves and daisy flower.

This is a plant you can literally ignore, maybe keep it watered and fed when you remember. Pick the leaves to make tea; just a couple in a cup of boiling water.

GROWING CHIVES

These are brilliant plants. You should buy lots of seeds each year. They look a little bit like grass, but they are little round tubes that grow to about 1ft (30cm), and give very pretty, spherical purple flowers. Simply scatter the seeds about the pots on the patio – I like to put a line of them around the outside of planters.

You can fill pots of any size – I don't bother to thin them out, just leave them to grow. When you need chives for cooking or salads you can simply go out with the scissors.

They will seed themselves and are biennial but I buy new seed every year.

GROWING DILL

This plant is a little like fennel and can be treated in exactly the same way, although in my experience it seeds at the end of its first summer. You can use the leaves and seeds in cooking – especially with trout. It is sometimes more convenient to buy young plants from the supermarket or garden centre, simply transplanting them to larger pots with fresh compost.

GROWING FEVERFEW

These plants resemble chamomile but they grow to about 1ft (30cm) high in 6 inch (15cm) pots of rich compost. Simply sow a few seeds per pot and thin out as they grow. They prefer full sun and apart from that they grow themselves.

GROWING LAVENDER

This plant needs full sun and should be well drained. It is better if you can grow it in a large tub (remember those ⅓ sawn off water butts?) of compost that is 70% rich compost, 20% well-rotted manure, and 10% sand. It likes good drainage but also likes to be watered well. If you feed it monthly it will colour up well and smell lovely.

You are probably best, because it's easiest, to buy plants and transfer them in April or May. Once you have a stand going in a tub they will last for years. Mine is eight years old and still going strong. You must remember to feed at least every three weeks during the growing period.

GROWING MARJORAM

Marjoram is a savoury herb that goes very well with all kinds of meat and is often described as being the very best herb for this purpose. Do consider adding marjoram, especially to steaks of beef, venison or lamb. It is also an excellent constituent of soups of all kinds.

Fresh plants do not do that well in the winter and they are best treated as annuals, sown each year. Grow them in pots of compost from seeds sown in April. Take leaves from June to November and bring inside before the first frosts. I tend to grow this fresh every two years. Water well in the summer and feed every three weeks.

GROWING MARIGOLD

This garden plant is edible. It makes a great addition to a salad and since you can use the flower as well as the leaf, you can add some surprising colour to an otherwise boring salad. In fact, the orange dye found in the petals is chemically the same as the orange in carrots.

The leaves are slightly peppery and fairly mild. Some people have been found to have an allergic reaction to the leaves, so try a small amount first to check. The problems are usually a swollen tongue, but it is a very rare event.

145

You can grow marigolds in pots. Sow indoors in March and outdoors in May. I use this plant all over the patio to disguise other food plants and generally brighten things up. Soak them in water before adding them to salads or sandwiches to give the insects a chance to get away and then dry them between pieces of kitchen paper. Serve it so that each person gets at least two petals each.

GROWING MUSTARD

Mustard is a member of the cabbage family and consequently full of sulphur. It is this ingredient that gives it its heat and healing properties. There are three types of mustard: black, white and brown, and a large amount of the countryside was once used for their propagation. White mustard is used in pickling spices and the other two are hotter, used in sauces and condiments.

Sow in trays and simply let them grow for mustard greens. However, transplant some of these to 6 inch (15cm) pots and let them grow out to get seeds for your own mustard. You need a dozen plants for a reasonable amount of seed. They ripen in September.

GROWING MINT

Apart from being obviously minty and extremely useful in the kitchen, mint is one of the most health giving plants there is, up there with the likes of garlic and onion. In this case, it is the digestive system that benefits. Mint aids the digestive system in fighting bacteria as well as easing the membranes that so easily become inflamed.

There are dozens of types of mint and they all share one irritating fact: they grow like mad! If you put a mint plant in the soil be aware that it will spread everywhere. The roots of the plant are very vigorous and within a few weeks you will be sick of the sight of them.

The best way to grow mint is to put it in 6 inch (15cm) plastic pots. It is easiest to buy a small plant from the supermarket and pot this on into larger ones with fresh compost. This way the roots are restricted and the plant will not out-grow its welcome. Apart from this, it is easy to grow. The flavour will be strengthened if you provide a feed of well-rotted compost in the spring and it will need to be kept well watered.

GROWING PARSLEY

Today parsley is the most commonly used herb in the world. There are three types.

Flat leaf parsley has large flat leaves and a strong flavour. *Curly parsley* has bright green, many lobed leaves and excellent flavour. *Turnip rooted parsley* is grown for its roots, which are reminiscent of celeriac.

Parsley is easy to grow from seed in moist compost: just broadcast seeds on a tray in spring and transplant to 3 inch (8cm) pots when the plants are big enough to handle, and then on to 6 inch (15cm) pots. If kept moderately warm, it grows quickly. Use rich compost and feed and water regularly.

GROWING ROSEMARY

This pleasantly pungent herb is named after rosmarinus, translated as 'the dew of the sea' and has nothing to do with roses or Mary. It is a powerfully astringent herb that produces some pretty violent responses in susceptible people, and has been used as a herb or in marinades for oily fish and meat.

It is a member of the mint family, though the pinnate leaves are borne on woody stems, and it doesn't resemble mint in flavour. The herb is used fresh and although slightly different, it is also dried to create a strong aromatic flavour.

People who have epilepsy should avoid taking this herb since it promotes seizures. The essential oil can induce anything from convulsions to nausea and vomiting, and should be avoided by anyone who has allergic reactions.

You can grow rosemary from cuttings. If you buy a 'living herb' from the supermarket or a pot from the garden centre, place it in a pot of good compost and keep it moist but not wet, in good sunlight. In the summertime cut out sprigs of leaves that do not bear flowers and simply stand the sprig into a small pot of moist compost. They should root easily and the following year you should have some decent little plants.

Rosemary is so strong that only a few leaves are needed, stripped off a single twig, scattered over lamb before roasting, in a marinade or a ragout. It is also used with game, particularly pheasant and veal and can be sprinkled on fish – particularly trout.

GROWING SAGE

Again sage is probably best bought as plants and simply transplanted into good quality compost in 12 inch (30cm) pots. It likes full sun and you will need to feed it fortnightly. In this way it will last around four years if you don't over pick it. The plant needs to be brought near the house in the winter, and on very cold days it is best to bring it indoors. Just take leaves as you want them. This herb has really beautiful flowers beloved by bumblebees.

GROWING THYME

This is one of the favourites of the garden. It is easy to grow but on the patio I suggest you get new plants every two years. You can grow from seeds sown in March indoors. I sow them in ordinary compost in modules and transplant the plants to 6 inch (15cm) pots and I restrict them to these around the patio. You need to grow lots around the patio. Bring them near the house in winter for added warmth.

GROWING VALERIAN AND VERBENA

These plants belong to the same family and are quite posionous in large quantities. You should not take them when pregnant or if you have liver problems or kidney problems, or blood pressure problems for that matter.

You can sow them in rich compost, but with no manure, sowing indoors in March. Transplant to 3 inch (8cm) pots and up to 12 inch (30cm) pots by June, when they can be placed outdoors.

GROWING VIOLET

You can buy packets of sweet violet seed and plant it in April indoors; it grows quite well, or in early summer you can buy it as a bedding plant. It will live for ever, but is best started new each year.

GROWING WINTER SAVOURY

Warming, wonderfully aromatic and completely underused, winter savoury is brilliant! It looks a little like thyme and grows well in pots. Sow in pots of compost (I use paper pots) and transplant the whole lot into a 12 inch (30cm) pot in April. Keep it indoors until the frost has gone in June.

You can keep the plant short and take it when you need it. If you grow this herb, leave it alone for a year and then it should crop for ever, especially if you trim it regularly. You can also buy it as plants and simply transplant them.

GROWING WATERCRESS

For those of you who believe this is only a garnish to be left on the side of your plate then think again! Watercress is probably one of the healthiest things you can eat!

Plant seeds in very moist compost in April. The plants are thinned to one good one per pot and then popped in a bucket of water, which can be changed every day. I tried to arrange a pipe from my roof downspout, but it didn't work too well. Then I found American land cress, which simply grows without fuss in compost pots.

CHAPTER 8

VARIETIES OF FRUIT AND VEGETABLES

DIFFERENT VARIETIES

Many of the varieties of fruit and vegetables I have grown on the patio have been with varying amounts of success. The point is, for pot growing, the smaller the better. Needless to say that any fruit on root stocks, like apples, pears etc., should be bought on dwarfing rootstocks.

Plant	Variety	Notes
Asparagus	'Good King Henry' 'Crimson Pacific'	The best cropper
Artichoke Globe	'Green Globe'	
Jerusalem Artichoke	'Fuseau'	
Aubergine	'Black Beauty' 'Snowy'	Best known variety A white variety
Broad Beans	'Bunyard's Exhibition'	The old-fashioned beans and still very good

French Beans	'Blue Lake'	
	'Tendergreen'	This is the dwarf one
Runner Beans	'Polestar'	Seems to crop forever
Beetroot	'Boltardy'	A great all-rounder
	'Burpees Golden'	
Broccoli	'Green Comet'	
	'Early Purple Sprouting'	This is the well known one – still good
Cabbage	'All Year Round'	This is the best one for patios and small spaces
Calabrese	'Long Season Cropping'	The most popular one often sold as broccoli
Carrot	'Early Nantes'	Old favourite
	'All Year Round'	
	'Resistafly'	Resistant to carrot root fly
Cauliflower	'Come and Cut Again'	Doesn't do well in pots
	'Snowball'	Excellent type
Celeriac	'Prinz'	
Celery	'Brydons Prize Red'	The old favourite
	'Golden Self Blanching'	Good for pots – compact
Chicory	'Brussels Wiltloof'	Strange name – good plant
Courgette	'Zucchini'	The main one – very good
	'Eight Ball'	Rounder shape – like a cricket ball
	'Taxi'	This is a yellow one
Cucumber	'Pyralis'	Compact one – very neat
Endive	'Salad King'	Curly variety
Fennel	'Sweet Florence'	
Garlic	'Purple Stripe'	Hardneck variety
	'Silverskin'	Softneck variety

Kale	'Dwarf Green'	
Leek	'Musselburgh'	Very hardy – doesn't mind being in a pot
Lettuce	'Lit' 'In Perpetuity' 'Cos'	A Lambs lettuce – really good in pots Cut-and-come-again The general purpose type
Onion	'Siberian Everlasting' 'White Lisbon' 'Sturon'	The Welsh type – really great for pots and you can grow them anywhere Good salad type The most common set variety
Parsnip	'Hamburg' 'Hollow Crown'	Not strictly a parsnip – but near enough The old favourite
Pea	'Douce Provance' 'Kelvedon Wonder' 'Carouby du Mausanne'	Quite compact The standard and very common type Mange tout variety
Potatoes	'Arran Pilot' 'Charlotte' 'Desiree' 'King Edward' 'Maris Piper' 'Pentland Types'	First Early Second Early Maincrop – red skinned Maincrop – general all rounder Great for Chips The best for the patio by far
Radish	'Rougette' 'Sparkler 3'	New variety that is very old fashioned Round one – very good – award winner
Rhubarb	'Victoria'	The old one – and probably the best
Shallot	'Matadoor' 'Golden Gourmet'	The best one on the patio
Spinach	'Little Grandad'	The original
Swede	'Brora' 'Best of all'	Probably true
Sweetcorn	'Swift Early' 'Popcorn'	A very quick maturing cob Baby sweetcorn, great fun for kids

Tomato	'Matts Wild Cherry'	Easy-to-grow cherry type
	'Shirley'	Early cropping
	'Moneymaker'	The standard good out and indoors
Turnip	'Snowball'	Nice and easy to grow
	'Purple Top'	Bigger, purple
Apple	'Discovery'	The standard
	'Stark's Earliest'	Very early fruiting
	'King of the Pippins'	The easiest to grow – brilliant fruit
Apricots	'Nancy'	Best of all for outdoors
Blackcurrant	'Ben Lomond'	The long-loved standard
Blueberry	'Jersey'	The standard plant
	'Bluecrop'	The newer, more popular easy to grow
Fig	'Brown Turkey'	The easiest to grow, and only one commonly available
Gooseberry	'Invicta'	Big plant – big fruit
	'Careless'	More compact – better disease resistance
Grape	'Black Hamburg'	The only one available once
	'Muller Thurgau'	A good outside variety
Kiwi	'Jenny'	Self fertile, smaller plant
Melon	'Charentais'	
	'Charlston Grey'	Best one for the UK
Peach	'Red Heaven'	
	'Darling'	Self fertile
Pear	'Clapps favourite'	Self fertile
	'Conference'	The UK standard
Raspberry	'Autumn Bliss'	The best ever – it's so easy to grow
	'Glen Cova'	
Strawberry	'Rambling Cascade'	Great for hanging baskets
	'Sweet Temptation'	Just the loveliest flavour

If I have missed out a variety – and this list is only a small one, it is because I haven't grown it or it's not much use on the patio. However, new varieties are grown every year, so please don't rely on the above information year in, year out!

INDEX